The Tet Offensive

➤ Battles of the Twentieth Century ◅

The Tet Offensive

by Earle Rice Jr.

Lucent Books, P.O. Box 289011, San Diego, CA 92198-9011

Library of Congress Cataloging-in-Publication Data

Rice, Earle.
    The Tet offensive / by Earle Rice, Jr.
      p.   cm. — (Battles of the twentieth century)
    Includes bibliographical references and index.
    Summary: Describes the planning, execution, and results of the
North Vietnamese army's major offensive in the Vietnam War.
    ISBN 1-56006-422-6 (alk. paper)
    1. Tet Offensive, 1968—Juvenile literature. [1. Tet Offensive, 1968.
2. Vietnamese Conflict, 1961–1975—Campaigns.] I. Title. II. Series.
DS557.8.T4R53   1997
959.704'342—dc20   96-14227
                                             CIP
                                             AC

Contents

Foreword

Almost everyone would agree with William Tecumseh Sherman that war "is all hell." Yet the history of war, and battles in particular, is so fraught with the full spectrum of human emotion and action that it becomes a microcosm of the human experience. Soldiers' lives are condensed and crystallized in a single battle. As Francis Miller explains in his *Photographic History of the Civil War* when describing the war wounded, "It is sudden, the transition from marching bravely at morning on two sound legs, grasping your rifle in two sturdy arms, to lying at nightfall under a tree with a member forever gone."

Decisions made on the battlefield can mean the lives of thousands. A general's pique or indigestion can result in the difference between life and death. Some historians speculate, for example, that Napoleon's fateful defeat at Waterloo was due to the beginnings of stomach cancer. His stomach pain may have been the reason that the normally decisive general was sluggish and reluctant to move his troops. And what kept George McClellan from winning battles during the Civil War? Some scholars and contemporaries believe that it was simple cowardice and fear. Others argue that he felt a gut-wrenching unwillingness to engage in the war of attrition that was characteristic of that particular conflict.

Battle decisions can be magnificently brilliant and horribly costly. At the Battle of Thaspus in 47 B.C., for example, Julius Caesar, facing a numerically superior army, shrewdly ordered his troops onto a narrow strip of land bordering the sea. Just as he expected, his enemy thought he had accidentally trapped himself and divided their forces to surround his troops. By dividing their army, his enemy had given Caesar the strategic edge he needed to defeat them. Other battle orders result in disaster, as in the case of the Battle at Balaklava during the Crimean War in 1854. A British general gave the order to attack a force of withdrawing enemy Russians. But confusion in relaying the order resulted in the 670 men of the Light Brigade's charging in the wrong direction into certain death by heavy enemy cannon fire. Battles are the stuff of history on the grandest scale—their outcomes often determine whether nations are enslaved or liberated.

Moments in battles illustrate the best and worst of human character. In the feeling of terror and the us-versus-them attitude that accompanies war, the enemy can be dehumanized and treated with a contempt that is considered repellent in times of peace. At Wounded Knee, the distrust and anticipation of violence that grew between the Native Americans and American soldiers led to the senseless killing of ninety men, women, and children. And who can forget My Lai, where the deaths of old men, women, and children at the hands of American soldiers shocked an America already disillusioned with the Vietnam War. The murder of six million Jews will remain burned into the human conscience forever as the measure of man's inhumanity to man. These horrors cannot be forgotten. And yet, under the terrible conditions of battle, one can find acts of bravery, kindness, and altruism. During the Battle of Midway, the members of Torpedo Squadron 8, flying in hopelessly antiquated planes and without the benefit of air protection from fighters, tried bravely to fulfill their mission—to destroy the *Kido Butai,* the Japanese Carrier Striking Force. Without air support, the squadron was immediately set upon by Japanese fighters. Nevertheless, each bomber tried valiantly to hit his target. Each failed. Every man but one died in the effort. But by keeping the Japanese fighters busy, the squadron bought time and delayed further Japanese fighter attacks. In the aftermath of the Battle of Isandhlwana in South Africa in 1879, a force of thousands of Zulu warriors trapped a contingent of British troops in a small trading post. After repeated bloody attacks in which many died on both sides, the Zulus, their final victory certain, granted the remaining British their lives as a gesture of respect for their bravery. During World War I, American troops were so touched by the fate of French war orphans that they took up a collection to help them. During the Civil War, soldiers of the North and South would briefly forget that they were enemies and share smokes and coffee across battle lines during the endless nights. These acts seem all the more dramatic, more uplifting, because they indicate that people can continue to behave with humanity when faced with inhumanity.

Lucent Books' Battles Series highlights the vast range of the human character revealed in the ordeal of war. Dramatic narrative describes in exciting and accurate detail the commanders, soldiers, weapons, strategies, and maneuvers involved in each battle. Each volume includes a comprehensive historical context, explaining what brought the parties to war, the events leading to the battle, what factors made the battle important, and the effects it had on the larger war and later events.

The Battles Series also includes a chronology of important dates that gives students an overview, at a glance, of each battle. Sidebars create a broader context by adding enlightening details on leaders, institutions, customs, warships, weapons, and armor mentioned in the narration. Every volume contains numerous maps that allow readers to better visualize troop movements and strategies. In addition, numerous primary and secondary source quotations drawn from both past historical witnesses and modern historians are included. These quotations demonstrate to readers how and where historians derive information about past events. Finally, the volumes in the Battles Series provide a launching point for further reading and research. Each book contains a bibliography designed for student research, as well as a second bibliography that includes the works the author consulted while compiling the book.

Above all, the Battles Series helps illustrate the words of Herodotus, the fifth-century B.C. Greek historian now known as the "father of history." In the opening lines of his great chronicle of the Greek and Persian Wars, the world's first battle book, he set for himself this goal: "To preserve the memory of the past by putting on record the astonishing achievements both of our own and of other peoples; and more particularly, to show how they came into conflict."

Chronology of Events

1954
May 7 The French stronghold at Dien Bien Phu falls to the Communist forces of North Vietnamese General Vo Nguyen Giap.

1955
November 1 The U.S. Military Assistance Advisory Group (MAAG) is formed to assist the Republic of (South) Vietnam.

1956
April 28 MAAG assumes responsibility for training the South Vietnamese forces.

1959
January North Vietnam's Central Executive Committee issues Resolution 15, changing North Vietnam's strategy toward South Vietnam from a "political struggle" to an "armed struggle."

July 8 Major Dale Buis and Master Sergeant Chester Ovnard become the first Americans killed in Vietnam.

1962
July The U.S. Army Special Forces—the Green Berets—establish a camp at Khe Sanh.

1965
April President Lyndon B. Johnson commits the first American combat troops to Vietnam.

1967
January General William C. Westmoreland orders the 3rd Marine Regiment and a navy Seabee battalion to build up defenses at Khe Sanh. The U.S. Special Forces move to nearby Lang Vei.

April 28–May 5 The "Hill Fights"; the 3rd Marines seize control of key hills around Khe Sanh in a series of battles with the NVA 325C Division.

May 13 The 1st Battalion, 26th Marines, relieves the 3rd Marines at Khe Sanh; the 2nd Battalion arrives one month later.

July The Politburo in Hanoi initiates planning and preparation for a "general offensive and general uprising" to force the United States out of the war and the collapse of the Thieu government.

August 14 Colonel David E. Lownds takes command of the 26th Marines at Khe Sanh.

September–October NVA and VC units suffer heavy losses in the northern provinces.

December Early in the month, marine and Special Forces reconnaissance patrols discover signs of increasing enemy activity around Khe Sanh.

December 20 General Westmoreland warns of a possible "maximum enemy effort over a relatively short period."

1968
January 2 Lima Company marines encounter six high-ranking NVA officers near Khe Sanh and kill five; one escapes.

January 13 Marine Task Force X-Ray established at Phu Bai.

January 17 The 2nd Battalion, 26th Marines, and a third 105mm battery of the 13th Marines arrive in Khe Sanh.

January 18–20 India Company marines engage NVA forces in heavy firefighting during reconnaissance patrols.

January 21 The NVA launches an all-out attack on the marine stronghold at Khe Sanh. General Westmoreland orders Operation Niagara bombings to commence. The siege of Khe Sanh begins.

January 22 The 1st Battalion, 9th Marines, arrives in Khe Sanh.

January 27 The 37th ARVN Ranger Battalion arrives in Khe Sanh.

January 30 The first day of the Tet holidays. Elements of the NVA and VC attack the cities of Nha Trang, Ban Me Thuot, Kontum, Hoi Nan, Da Nang, Qui Nhon, and Pleiku.

January 31 The Tet Offensive commences in earnest throughout South Vietnam. Communist forces assault Saigon and Hue, and, in total, 36 of 44 provincial capitals, 5 of 6 autonomous cities, 64 of 242 district capitals, and 23 airfields or bases. Alpha Company, 1st Battalion, 1st Marines, reinforces besieged MACV compound in Hue; a second relief force led by Lieutenant Colonel Marcus J. Gravel arrives in Hue that afternoon. The reinforced 3rd Regiment of the 1st ARVN Division fights its way into the city and joins besieged ARVN troops in the Citadel late in the day.

February 1–3 Marines fight holding action in New City (Hue); 2nd Battalion, 5th Marines, under Lieutenant Colonel Ernest C. Cheatham, arrives in New City.

February 2 The 3rd Brigade of the U.S. Army's 1st Air Cavalry Division air assaults into an LZ six miles northwest of Hue, then seizes an enemy-held hill four miles west of Hue. The brigade's 5th Battalion, 7th Cavalry, sweeps in from west of Hue to attempt a linkup with the 2nd Battalion.

February 4 Second Battalion marines launch an attack to regain control of New City.

February 5 Echo Company marines repel enemy attack on Hill 861 Alpha.

February 6 Hotel Company marines tear down the Vietcong flag and hoist the American flag, "Old Glory," at the Thua Thien Provincial headquarters in New City.

February 7 American and ARVN troops clear Saigon of all but small, isolated enemy units. The special forces camp at Lang Vei attacked by NVA tanks and ground troops.

February 8 Lang Vei falls.

February 9 The 3rd Brigade's 2nd Battalion assaults the village of Thong Bon Tri and clears the area of NVA troops. Colonel Stanley S. Hughes, regimental commander of the 1st Marines, takes charge of all marine operations south of the Perfume River. The 1st Battalion, 9th Marines, surrenders Hill 64 near Khe Sanh in the dark; the marines counterattack and recapture Hill 64 in the daylight.

February 11 Hotel Company holds a bridgehead on the west bank of the Phu Cam Canal.

February 12 The 1st Battalion, 5th Marines, enters the Old City (Hue) from the north by helicopter and landing craft.

February 20 Alpha Company, 1st Battalion, 5th Marines, takes a key tower on the northeast wall of the Citadel.

February 21 First Battalion marines secure the northeast wall of the Citadel and—for a second time—hoist Old Glory over liberated South Vietnamese soil. Elements of the U.S. 1st Air Cavalry Division close in on Hue from the west and south and sever the last remaining supply route. The 37th ARVN Ranger Battalion repels NVA attack on its positions at Khe Sanh.

February 23 Allied troops regain control of Saigon suburbs. A patrol from Bravo Company is ambushed by the enemy near Khe Sanh with heavy losses.

February 24 The Black Panther Company of the 1st ARVN Division's 2nd Battalion, 3rd Regiment, runs down the NLF flag and raises the South Vietnamese colors at the Midday Gate of the Imperial Palace in Hue. The Tet Offensive officially ends.

February 29 The 37th ARVN Ranger Battalion again repulses an NVA attack at Khe Sanh.

April 1 Operation Pegasus commences.

April 6 Marines and ARVN units pushing out from Khe Sanh link up with elements of the U.S. 1st Air Cavalry Division, the 1st Marine Division, and the South Vietnamese Airborne Brigade.

April 8 The 3rd Brigade of the 1st Air Cavalry Division officially relieves the marines. The siege of Khe Sanh ends.

April 14 The 3rd Battalion, 26th Marines, seize Hill 881 North.

June U.S. troops abandon the Khe Sanh Combat Base.

INTRODUCTION

"General Offensive, General Uprising"

*S*hortly after midnight on January 31, 1968, nineteen members of the South Vietnamese National Liberation Front (NLF)—better known to the world as Vietcong (VC)—secretly assembled in a garage about five blocks away from the American Embassy in Saigon. They sat huddled together in silence, cleaning and oiling their weapons, listening to final instructions from their leaders on their forthcoming commando-style operation.

At 0230, they boarded waiting vehicles, carrying Soviet-pattern 7.62mm AK-47 assault rifles and B-40 rockets and C 4 plastic explosive charges. Most of the VC climbed into the back of a Peugeot truck. The rest piled into a run-down taxicab. They then proceeded slowly to the intersection of Mac Dinh Chi Street and Thong Nhut Boulevard. As they traveled the five blocks to the American Embassy, all nineteen men shared a common thought: probably not one among them would survive the night.

They reached the intersection at 0247, rounded the corner, and opened fire on two American MPs (military police) guarding the embassy gate. Army Specialist Fourth Class Daniel and Private First Class Sebast fired back, hitting at least two Vietcong, then clanged the embassy's steel gate shut.

One of the MPs radioed "Signal 300"—a code name indicating distress. Moments later, the Vietcong raiders scaled the eight-foot embassy walls and gunned down Daniel and Sebast. Inside the modern, six-story building—a $2.6 million monument to the American presence in Vietnam—only three marine security guards remained on duty to defend the embassy. . . .

In such sudden violence began the Tet Offensive.

Tet—the Lunar New Year—is the most important of Vietnamese holidays. By American standards, a combined celebration of Thanksgiving, Christmas, New Year's, and the Fourth of July would represent a fair comparison. To the Vietnamese, Tet marks a time for renewal, family gatherings, and ancestral worship. During the three days of its celebration, Tet reaches beyond all classes and religions. All people rejoice in perfect harmony. The date of its observance varies, depending on the phase of the moon.

In 1968, Tet commenced on January 30—the first day of the hopeful new Year of the Monkey.

Master of the Art

During the Vietnam War, troops on both sides traditionally laid down their arms in favor of a mutually agreed upon three-day cease-fire honoring the Tet holidays. Insofar as the Army of the Republic of (South) Vietnam (ARVN) was concerned, 1968 was to have been no exception. The North Vietnamese Army (NVA)—sometimes known as the People's Army of (North) Vietnam (PAVN)—and the Vietcong (South Vietnamese communist guerrillas) had other ideas. As the Year of the Monkey drew near, North Vietnam was preparing to launch a massive, simultaneous assault against nearly every major population center and military installation in South Vietnam.

The fall of the French stronghold at Dien Bien Phu on May 7, 1954, had effectively marked the end of nearly a century of French rule in Vietnam. During the next eight years, Vietcong rebels conducted continuous guerrilla activities designed to overthrow the South Vietnamese government. North Vietnam, under the Communist regime of Ho Chi Minh, supported the VC operations with troops and equipment. Communist China, in turn, supported North Vietnam with war matériel.

Fearing a communist takeover in Southeast Asia, the United States decided to assist the Republic of Vietnam by pouring aid into the country in steadily increasing amounts. The U.S. Military Assistance Advisory Group (MAAG)—formed on November 1, 1955, to provide assistance to the Republic of Vietnam—assumed responsibility for training South Vietnamese forces on April 28, 1956. Meanwhile, Vietcong guerrilla activities rose steadily.

Since April 1965, when President Lyndon B. Johnson had committed the first American combat troops to Vietnam (other than military "advisers"), North Vietnam had fought the enormously powerful forces of the United States to a virtual standstill. They had hoped by means of a protracted, or prolonged, struggle to wear down American determination to continue the fight. By 1967, however, just the opposite seemed to be happening. The Americans had bolstered the strength of their forces in Vietnam from 760 military advisers in 1959 to 485,600 troops in 1967. And

Military Twenty-Four-Hour Clock

Military times are used throughout the book. This key, showing familiar A.M. and P.M. times paired with the corresponding time on the twenty-four-hour clock, may be helpful in learning the system.

A.M.	24	P.M.	24
1	0100	1	1300
2	0200	2	1400
3	0300	3	1500
4	0400	4	1600
5	0500	5	1700
6	0600	6	1800
7	0700	7	1900
8	0800	8	2000
9	0900	9	2100
10	1000	10	2200
11	1100	11	2300
12	1200	12	2400

President Lyndon B. Johnson shakes hands with American troops during his 1966 visit to Vietnam. By the following year, the U.S. government had committed a total of 485,600 troops to the war against North Vietnam.

General Vo Nguyen Giap was the mastermind behind the important Tet Offensive, which would prove to be a risky campaign for the North Vietnamese.

they appeared well on their way toward winning the battle for the "hearts and minds" of the South Vietnamese people.

In July 1967, the Politburo in Hanoi took steps to shatter American confidence and to force the United States out of the war. At the same time, they hoped to induce the collapse of the South Vietnamese government, then headed by President Nguyen Van Thieu.

North Vietnam's defense minister, General Vo Nguyen Giap, took personal charge of the planning, preparation, coordination, and execution of the biggest and boldest offensive operation of the Vietnam War. Giap, the principal architect of the Vietminh's dramatic victory over French forces at Dien Bien Phu, sensed the potential for another great triumph.

"The opportunity for a general offensive and general uprising is within reach," Giap told his fellow Politburo members. "We shall coordinate attacks, and the local population will rise up to take over." He added that his troops would "undermine the government of the South by attacking towns and cities."

Giap's plan for coordinated attacks across the length and breadth of South Vietnam was boldly ambitious and extremely risky. The success of the operation would rely heavily on secrecy and surprise—vital elements in the art of war. Maintaining secrecy and achieving surprise would require careful planning, enormous preparation, and near-faultless execution. Masterminding and directing an event of such far-reaching consequence represented a formidable challenge, even for the hero of Dien Bien Phu. A failed offensive of this size would greatly diminish the Communists' ability to keep fighting and could result in a lost war. Giap advanced his plan slowly, methodically, and very carefully. The general was a master of the art of war.

Setting the Stage

In August 1967, following Hanoi's decision to proceed with Giap's "General Offensive, General Uprising," the general began a massive buildup of troops, equipment, and supplies in South

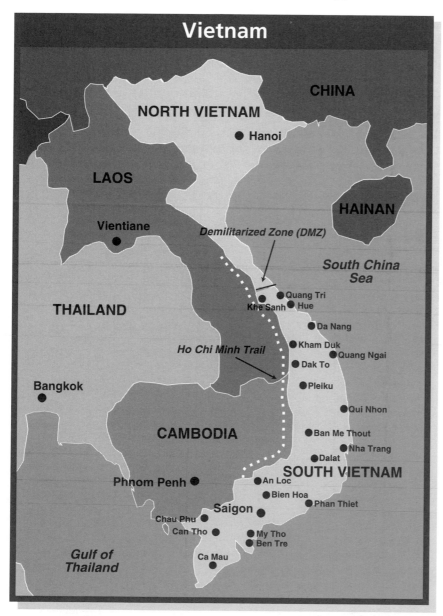

The Vietminh

The Revolutionary League for the Independence of Vietnam, or Vietminh—the abbreviated form of *Viet Nam Doc-Lap Dong Minh*—was an alliance of Vietnamese Communist and Nationalist parties headed by the Communist leader Ho Chi Minh. Formed by Ho in 1941, the Communist-dominated military and political organization first gained recognition through its determined resistance effort against Japanese occupation forces during World War II. In time, the Vietminh earned the respect and trust of the United States and the support of the U.S. Office of Strategic Services (OSS).

Upon Japan's surrender on September 2, 1945, Ho Chi Minh proclaimed Vietnam's independence from France's prewar colonial rule and established the Democratic Republic of Vietnam. But the French, unwilling to give up their Vietnamese colonies, moved back into Vietnam after the war. The Vietminh guerrillas then engaged French colonial forces in an eight-year struggle for Vietnamese independence. That struggle, which came to be known as the First Indochina War, ended shortly after the Vietminh's stunning defeat of the French at Dien Bien Phu on May 7, 1954.

When the war with the French ended, Vietminh guerrillas in what was to become South Vietnam numbered about ninety thousand. Most of them returned to their homes in the north. But some ten thousand guerrillas remained in the south to form a core group of covert Communist organizers and agents.

In 1959, North Vietnam's Politburo ordered the former Vietminh rebels to begin active guerrilla operations with the intent of overthrowing the standing South Vietnamese government. These guerrillas became known as *Vietnam Cong San* (Vietnamese Communists), or simply Vietcong, and the Second Indochina War began.

As the head of the Revolutionary League for the Independence of Vietnam, Ho Chi Minh (pictured) lead his Vietminh guerrillas to victory during the First Indochina War.

Vietnam. Thousands of tons of guns and munitions flowed southward along the Ho Chi Minh Trail—the vital Vietcong supply line that snaked through the jungles of North Vietnam, down across the mountains of Laos and eastern Cambodia. Transported by truck, bicycle, oxcart, and sampan and on the backs of soldiers, guerrillas, and laborers, tons of food and medical supplies were moved south and stored in "safe houses" and villages scattered throughout South Vietnam.

Tens of thousands of troops poured down from the north and infiltrated the countryside or, wearing civilian clothes, blended with the local populace. They took up positions near cities and military bases across the land. Targeted cities included Saigon, Da Nang, Hue, Kontum, Ban Me Thuot, Phan Thiet, Can Tho, and Ben Tre, to name but a few.

By mid-January 1968, an estimated eighty-four thousand NVA and VC troops were deployed in South Vietnam. Two weeks before the holidays, Giap's forces stood positioned and ready for an attack against thirty-six provincial capitals, sixty-four district capitals, five other cities, and more than twenty military installations. The stage was set for Tet.

The Evidence Mounts

Contrary to the popular misconception that the Tet Offensive took the Americans by complete surprise, it did not. American intelligence sources had started uncovering evidence that indicated a shift in enemy strategy in the late summer and early fall of 1967. One key indicator came in the form of a captured NVA attack order, seized by a unit of the 101st Airborne Division while operating in Quang Tin Province on November 19.

The order echoed Giap's earlier words to the Politburo: "Central Headquarters concludes that the time has come for direct revolution and that the opportunity for a general offensive and general uprising is within reach." The captured document went on to outline key elements of the forthcoming offensive:

> Use very strong military attacks in coordination with the uprisings of the local population to take over towns and cities. Troops should flood the lowlands. They should move toward liberating the capital city [Saigon], take power, and try to rally enemy [ARVN] brigades and regiments to our side one by one. Propaganda should be broadly disseminated among the population in general, and leaflets should be used to reach enemy officers and enlisted men.

In this brief paragraph, the attack order diagrammed the basics of the enemy's new strategy and heralded the imminence of a large-scale offensive. Unfortunately, U.S. military intelligence officers regarded this revealing information as nothing more than

Phonetic Alphabet

The phonetic alphabet used by the U.S. military was created to prevent potentially serious communication errors. For example, the letters "C," "D," and "E" sound similar when heard via radio communication. By using designated words that begin with each letter of the alphabet, confusion is avoided.

Alpha
Bravo
Charlie
Delta
Echo
Foxtrot
Golf
Hotel
India
Juliet
Kilo
Lima
Mike
November
Oscar
Papa
Quebec
Romeo
Sierra
Tango
Uniform
Victor
Whiskey
X-Ray
Yankee
Zulu

Marines wait to board helicopters shortly before the Tet Offensive. The allied forces of the United States and South Vietnam appeared to be winning the war; however, a massive enemy assault loomed on the horizon.

enemy propaganda, intended to lift NVA and VC troop morale. Even when the document was published on January 5, it failed to attract serious attention.

As 1967 drew to a close, the United States appeared to be winning the war. A feeling of guarded optimism prevailed among government leaders and the news media. But the growing evidence of a major enemy attack in the offing had not gone unnoticed by American officials in Washington and Saigon.

In Washington, on December 18, General Earle G. Wheeler, chairman of the Joint Chiefs of Staff, cautioned that "it is entirely possible that there may be a Communist thrust similar to the desperate effort of the Germans in the Battle of the Bulge in World War II."

In Saigon, two days later, General William C. Westmoreland, U.S. Army (USA), commander of the U.S. Military Assistance Command, Vietnam (MACV), expressed a similar view. Westmoreland cabled Washington that he expected the North Vietnamese Army and the Vietcong "to undertake an intensified countrywide effort, perhaps a maximum effort over a relatively short period."

On that same day, December 20, President Lyndon B. Johnson warned: "We face dark days ahead." The president, expecting the worst from a desperate enemy, warned that the North Vietnamese and Vietcong might soon resort to "kamikaze tactics" and launch "a wave of suicide attacks."

In early January 1968, American forces captured a pair of NVA operations orders. One order called for an attack on Pleiku prior to Tet; the other, without specifying a date, targeted Ban Me Thuot for assault.

Two days before Tet, agents of the South Vietnamese Military Security Service arrested eleven Vietcong leaders caught holding a secret meeting in Qui Nhon. In the VCs' possession were found two tapes containing recorded messages for radio broadcast to the people. The messages announced the "liberation" of Saigon, Hue, and other South Vietnamese cities and appealed for the people to take up arms against the South Vietnamese government.

Many early warnings of an impending offensive were either discounted or ignored. One U.S. intelligence officer recalled, "If we'd gotten the whole battle plan, it wouldn't have been believed. It wouldn't have been credible to us." Intelligence analysts within MACV simply refused to believe that the NVA and VC were capable of executing such a large-scale, coordinated attack.

At first, General Westmoreland himself had all but dismissed the notion of a countrywide enemy offensive, referring to it as "suicidal." He reasoned that enemy forces, so dispersed, could not concentrate sufficient force to gain a single objective. Moreover, thinly spread, they would multiply their own points of vulnerability. As evidence of the approaching offensive continued to mount, however, Westmoreland changed his reasoning.

Suspicions Confirmed

By mid-January, Westmoreland felt sure that the predicted offensive would commence either just before or just after the Tet holidays. His chief intelligence officer, Brigadier General Phillip B. Davidson, agreed. Because Tet is basically a time for religious devotion, both generals discounted the possibility of an enemy strike *during* the holidays. And both generals still doubted the enemy's ability to strike in so many places at once. In time, the anticipated attack became not so much a question of when but rather of *where*.

General William C. Westmoreland (pictured), commander of the U.S. Military Assistance Command in Vietnam, addresses soldiers stationed in Saigon.

The Ho Chi Minh Trail

Throughout the Vietnam War, the North Vietnamese denied sending troops into South Vietnam, maintaining that the fighting was being conducted entirely by "southern revolutionaries." In truth, tens of thousands of NVA troops, thousands of vehicles, and untold tons of equipment and supplies entered South Vietnam via the Ho Chi Minh Trail, beginning as early as 1959.

This "trail" originated in North Vietnam and ran south along the mountains of the Chaîne Annamitque. Twisting through the Laotian panhandle and eastern border regions of Cambodia, it branched off into several trunk lines. These spurs terminated in key base areas in South Vietnam, such as the A Shau Valley, the Ia Drang Valley, and the Mekong Delta.

Restricted by U.S. policy from entering North Vietnam, Laos, and Cambodia, the U.S. and ARVN forces were unable to sever this vital Communist supply line. By the time of the final NVA offensive in 1975, the Ho Chi Minh Trail had grown to resemble an expressway. The commander of that last offensive, NVA General Van Tien Dung, described the trail this way:

> The strategic route east of the Truong Son Range [the Ho Chi Minh Trail] was the result of the labor of more than 30,000 troops and shock youths. The length of this route, added to that of the other old and new strategic routes used during various campaigns built during the last war, is more than 20,000 kms [kilometers] [12,500 miles]. The eight-meter [26.4 feet] wide route of more than 1,000 kms [625 miles], which we could see now, is our pride. With 5,000 kms [3,125 miles] of pipeline laid through deep rivers and streams and on mountains more than 1,000 meters [3,300 feet] high, we were capable of providing enough fuel for various battlefronts. More than 10,000 transportation vehicles were put on the road [during the final offensive].

The Ho Chi Minh Trail has been described often and aptly as North Vietnam's "road to victory."

During the fall of 1967, NVA and VC units had suffered heavy losses during several engagements with U.S. and ARVN forces. In September, marines, supported by airpower, naval gunfire, and artillery, repulsed two NVA battalions at Con Thien, killing more than two thousand enemy soldiers. In October, ARVN troops, aided by American artillery and airpower, fought off the 88th NVA Regiment at Song Be, and the 273rd Vietcong Regiment at Loc Ninh, dispatching over one thousand more enemy troops in the two battles. In another confrontation beginning on October 27 and continuing for twenty-two days, nine U.S. battalions and six ARVN battalions engaged four NVA regiments in the Dak To area. The American and South Vietnamese troops killed over sixteen hundred more enemy soldiers, virtually destroying the four NVA regiments.

In the aftermath of these losses, a massive enemy offensive in January seemed unlikely indeed. Westmoreland and his advisers concluded that a more focused attack against South Vietnam's two northernmost provinces, Quang Tri and Thua Thien, represented a more workable—and thus a more likely—enemy option.

Operating close to their main supply bases in Laos, North Vietnam, and the demilitarized zone (DMZ)—a six-mile-wide neutral zone along the 17th parallel, separating North and South Vietnam—the NVA and VC would minimize their supply problems. Furthermore, they would remain within a short distance of safe haven should events dictate a hasty withdrawal.

Enemy documents naming the old imperial capital city of Hue as a principal objective seemed to affirm Westmoreland's thinking. Also, the general suspected that the enemy might soon attempt to overrun the marine stronghold at Khe Sanh, in an effort to achieve a Dien Bien Phu–style triumph. He decided to reduce his own offensive operations and began stiffening his northern defenses.

Westmoreland's suspicions seemed to gain confirmation when an enemy force of somewhere between fifteen and twenty thousand troops launched an all-out attack on the marines at Khe Sanh on January 21, 1968.

At last, the enemy's long-threatened "General Offensive, General Uprising" had come. Or had it?

CHAPTER ONE

Before Tet: Battles at the Border

Lieutenant General Lewis W. Walt, commander of the 3rd Marine Division and the III Marine Amphibious Force (III MAF) in Vietnam, once called the siege of Khe Sanh between January 21 and April 8, 1968, "the most important battle of the war." Probably more than a few military analysts would dispute Walt's appraisal. But no amount of argument can detract from the spirit of cooperation, determination, and courage demonstrated by the defenders of the marine stronghold at Khe Sanh.

U.S. Marines assume defensive positions while the North Vietnamese Army bombards the hills near the combat base at Khe Sanh.

"I had the finest enlisted men in the world. And they had the best morale, under the conditions, that *any* commander could ask for," recalled Colonel David E. Lownds, commander of the U.S. Marine Corps garrison at Khe Sanh. "Since January 21, there was no hot chow, no beer, and no showers available. But every Marine I saw had a smile on his face. To them goes all the credit."

First Attack

The first attack at Khe Sanh came on January 21, 1968. At about half past midnight, elements of the North Vietnamese 325 Division launched an assault against Hill 861, a marine outpost northwest of the main combat base. Marines of Kilo Company, 3rd Battalion, 26th Marines, engaged more than three hundred attackers in a desperate defense of their outpost.

At one point during the fighting, Sergeant Michael R. Stahl, a forward observer for the 4.2-inch mortars of the 1st Battalion, 13th Marines, called for star shells to light up the battle zone. "You could see hundreds and hundreds of NVA coming up our hill, up the slopes," Stahl recalled later. "They were yelling, firing. It looked kind of like a football game where you [are] observing it from the air."

The 1st Platoon, defending the hill's northwest corner, caught the brunt of the attack. Lieutenant Linn Oehling's 2nd Platoon, covering the helicopter landing zone (LZ) lower on the hill, had yet to come under attack. Oehling sent six marines up the hill to help plug holes in 1st Platoon's defenses. They hastened up the hill but returned promptly to Oehling's position.

"Lieutenant, they're shooting us!"

No kidding, Oehling thought. He then told his troopers, "It's not a one-way war; you can fire back at 'em!"

"You want us to go back up there?"

"You got small arms and you got grenades," Oehling answered. "Use the best tactics you know and kick the [deleted] out of 'em!"

The six marines scrambled back up the hill, killed three North Vietnamese soldiers while recapturing a section of the marine trench line, and held doggedly to their newly recovered positions throughout the assault.

"I can't tell you how proud of them I was," a pleased Oehling said later. "No one likes to do a job like that; somebody has to do it. And they did a fine job."

The Kilo Company marines managed to repel the hordes of NVA attackers, but only after savage fighting that lasted until 0630 that morning.

At 0530, while the opening battle on Hill 861 raged on, North Vietnamese artillery and mortars commenced blasting away at the main base at Khe Sanh. A rain of fire ripped holes in the aluminum matting covering the airstrip's 3,900-foot runway. An ammunition dump containing fifteen hundred tons of munitions broke out in flames and exploded. The huge blast demolished a helicopter, killed eighteen marines, and wounded forty more. Terror and chaos ruled the moment.

"It was a nightmare," recalled Lance Corporal Dennis Jennings. "One minute I was sitting behind my machine gun waiting

Carrying weapons and supplies, marines charge from a helicopter landing zone in the hills near Khe Sanh Combat Base.

A God-Forsaken Place

General William C. Westmoreland regarded Khe Sanh as a key element in his grand battle scheme and insisted on maintaining a strong force at the remote combat base. Many marine commanders, believing that the base was too isolated to supply and support efficiently, resisted Westmoreland's plan. A notable critic was General Lowell English, assistant commander of the 3rd Marine Division, which would eventually have to defend the distant site. English later recalled his objections with piercing clarity:

> If we put a battalion at Khe Sanh I knew that in a month we would have to reinforce it with an entire regiment. Before you can hold Khe Sanh, you first have to occupy and hold the prominent terrain features in the area; most notably Hills 881 North and South, and Hill 861. To hold those three hills alone would take a battalion by itself, plus one battery of artillery for each hill. But even if you held Khe Sanh, what would you have? Nothing, that's what. There's nothing out there. And even if you lost it, you haven't lost a damn thing! The only reason there was a battle in that God-forsaken place was because Westmoreland wanted it!

for the enemy to attack, and the next thing I knew I was flat on my back with my machine gun nowhere in sight." He went on:

> When the ammo dump went I was more afraid of getting killed by one of our own rounds than of being hit by the enemy. In fact, I forgot all about the NVA shelling. After the first explosion, I got up and was running as hard as I could when another explosion rocked the base. I saw a foxhole about ten feet in front of me and dove headfirst into it. Then the shock wave hit and threw me out of that hole just like I was a piece of paper. I got to my feet again and headed for a bunker. When I got inside, I felt this stinging sensation on my arms and face. I looked down, and my flak jacket was covered with steel fléchettes [darts]. My arms were bleeding, and I felt blood running down my face. At that moment I said a prayer and thanked God that Colonel Lownds had made us wear our flak jackets. If he hadn't, I would have looked like a piece of swiss cheese.

A series of secondary explosions from the first awesome blast continued for another forty-eight hours.

Seventy-Seven Days

The NVA launched their first daylight assault against nearby Khe Sanh village. The village was only lightly defended by the marines of Combined Action Company (CAC) Oscar, the regional American advisory group; and by Regional Force troops, local South Vietnamese units assigned to village defense. With his combat base severely understaffed and under siege and having already lost most of his ammunition, Colonel Lownds could do little to assist the village defenders. Although Lownds slowed the enemy advance by directing a storm of artillery fire against the NVA attackers, the village had to be abandoned the next morning.

Meanwhile, the Khe Sanh defenders—all three infantry battalions of the 26th Marines, and the 1st Artillery Battalion of the 13th Marines—burrowed into their prepared positions. (The physical limits of the compound itself restricted the marine garrison at Khe Sanh to about six thousand defenders. At the start of the siege, the entire garrison numbered about thirty-five hundred marines. The 1st Battalion, 9th Marines, and the 37th ARVN Ranger Battalion—airlifted in during the first week of hostilities—increased the defense ranks to slightly more than the limit of six thousand.) And the siege of Khe Sanh began. It would last for seventy-seven days.

Khe Sanh Combat Base

The U.S. Army Special Forces—the Green Berets—had set up the camp at Khe Sanh in 1962. It had served as an in-country base from which the soldiers could probe and patrol the network of roads and trails used by the enemy to move troops and supplies into the area. Not until 1966 did the North Vietnamese tire of U.S. operations there and begin to shell the camp.

In January 1967, as a result of increased Communist pressure on Khe Sanh, MACV chief General William C. Westmoreland ordered the 3rd Marine Regiment and a navy Seabee battalion to Khe Sanh. The task of clearing the area of NVA and Vietcong fell to the marines while the Seabees were to rebuild an old French airstrip and further strengthen base defenses. To make room for the marines, the Special Forces reluctantly moved their camp westward to the nearby montagnard village of Lang Vei.

The Khe Sanh Combat Base (KSCB) was built on a low plateau, nestled among jungle-covered hills colored a lush green by monsoon rains and lingering fog and mist. Located about fifteen miles south of the DMZ, near the Laotian border, Khe Sanh anchored the western end of a string of combat bases that stretched across the narrow northern neck of South Vietnam. The string ran parallel to Route 9, the main through road from Laos to the key cities of Quang Tri and Hue. Khe Sanh Combat Base

(Left) An aerial photograph shows the guns and fortifications of the 3rd Marine Regiment at Khe Sanh Combat Base. (Below) A U.S. Marine patrol advances toward Khe Sanh along Route 9, the main thoroughfare between Laos and Hue.

Second-Guessing Giap

General William C. Westmoreland, MACV commander during the Tet Offensive of 1968, was often asked if he saw himself in a personal contest with General Vo Nguyen Giap. The general answered the often-asked question later in writing:

> I have always tried to put myself in my adversary's position, to see myself through his eyes. I frequently did this with Giap. . . .
>
> President Johnson asked me in 1966, "If you were Giap, what would you do in Vietnam?" I told him I would attack across the DMZ, overrun Khe Sanh, go through the A Shau Valley and isolate the two northernmost provinces with a sweep through the Hai Van Pass to capture Hue, the old capital. Quang Tri and Thua Thien provinces, the two northernmost provinces, were very exposed at the time. We had only two small airfields up there and no deepwater port. Now, I was trying to think the way Giap did, so before the Tet offensive I reinforced the marines with three army divisions [in the I Corps sector], built airfields and hardstands for helicopters, and developed port facilities. I was getting ready for an attack based on an analysis of what Giap could do, and so we were prepared for him when it came. Unfortunately, it's not obvious to the American people to this day that we stopped him in his tracks during Tet.

overlooked Route 9 and stood like a rock in the path of North Vietnamese intruders. Farther to the east, the 175mm guns of two army fire bases called Rockpile and Camp J. J. Carroll lent welcome support to the Khe Sanh garrison.

Of the hills surrounding Khe Sanh, Hills 881 North, 881 South, and 861 (named for their height in meters) to the west and north of the combat base were the most important. Within view of the plateau, all three hills overlooked the Rao Quan River, a likely approach route for NVA forces attacking from the northwest.

The Hill Fights

American military commanders had long held to the idea of luring the NVA into a set-piece battle—that is, a carefully planned and executed military operation. They felt that, given the time and place of their choosing, the full fury of unleashed American artillery and aerial firepower would destroy the NVA and probably end the war. Details of this concept remained privileged to only a few top-level strategists. Khe Sanh gained frequent mention among them as a likely site for this type of decisive confrontation.

But before the Americans could use Khe Sanh for a set-piece battle, they would first have to command the strategically located hills to the west and north of the base. Accordingly, following several NVA ambushes of marine patrols around Hill 861, the marines initiated the first major fighting in the Khe Sanh area, almost a year before the siege.

From April 28 through May 5, 1967, the 2nd and 3rd Battalions of Colonel John P. Lanigan's 3rd Marine Regiment attacked elements of the NVA 325C Division and seized control of Hills 881 North, 881 South, and 861. In that series of savage battles, thereafter known as the Hill Fights, the marines paid a high price, incurring 155 dead and 425 wounded.

The official marine history for that period characterizes the battles with brief understatement, noting that "the cost of stopping the Communist effort was not light."

(Above) Marine tank crews watch as American aircraft strafe the hills outside of Khe Sanh Combat Base, where the U.S. and South Vietnamese troops battled the North Vietnamese. (Left) Protected by a bunker, marines fire at Communist snipers.

On May 13, 1967, Colonel John J. Padley's 1st Battalion, 26th Marines, relieved Lanigan's 3rd Marines. The 3rd Battalion, 26th Marines, arrived at Khe Sanh a month later. Colonel David E. Lownds, a veteran of marine campaigns on Kwajalein, Saipan, and Iwo Jima during World War II, flew in on August 14 to take command of the 26th Marines and the garrison. Padley went home.

The Calm Before

A period of relative calm followed the Hill Fights. Because of more pressing needs for troops elsewhere, the Marine Corps reduced its presence in the Khe Sanh area. It abandoned Hill 881 North and left only company-sized elements on 881 South and 861. "Enemy units practically disappeared from the area, and there was little activity for several months," wrote Major Mark A. Swearingen, USA, an artillery coordinator for the nearby Rockpile and Camp Carroll fire bases. The marines and Seabees used the slack period to shore up defenses, dig trenches, construct bunkers, improve artillery positions, and upgrade the airstrip to accept the big C-130 transports. The giant cargo planes would be used later to airlift vital supplies into the isolated combat base. Their hard work would later save many lives.

Looking for a Fight

In early December, marine and Special Forces reconnaissance patrols discovered signs of increasing NVA activity around Khe Sanh. Enemy units that had earlier moved through the area now appeared to be staying. The stubborn NVA 325C Division, which the 3rd Marines had defeated during the Hill Fights, was back with renewed strength. Further reports indicated the presence of the NVA 304th Division, assembling nearby to the southwest. These two divisions alone fielded about twenty thousand troops.

Furthermore, the NVA 320th and 324th Divisions were within twenty-five kilometers (about fifteen and a half miles) of Khe Sanh and could lend quick assistance if needed. All of these divisions were reported to be heavily equipped with artillery, mortars, and rockets in a wide range of shapes and sizes. Intelligence gurus anticipated that this array of weaponry would soon be brought to bear on the Khe Sanh Combat Base.

On December 7, 1967, Joint Chiefs chairman General Earle G. Wheeler, perhaps fearing a Pearl Harbor–like attack on Khe Sanh, cabled General Westmoreland. Wheeler's cable asked a series of questions about the MACV commander's strategy regarding the marine base that now appeared to be threatened by gathering NVA forces.

Because of the adverse psychological, political, and economic effects of abandoning Khe Sanh in the face of an enemy buildup, Westmoreland discounted withdrawal as an option. In a cabled response to Wheeler on December 10, Westmoreland stated that a withdrawal would also be "unsound from a military standpoint." He stressed the importance of aggressively challenging all enemy intrusions into South Vietnam:

> If we do not violently contest every attempt to get NVA units into South Vietnam, we permit him to expand his system of bases in-country. . . . When we engage the enemy near the borders we often preempt his plans and force him to fight before he is fully organized.

> When the enemy moves across the borders we must strike him as soon as he is within reach, and before he can gain a victory or tyrannize the local population. We cannot permit him to strike the confidence of the South Vietnamese people in ultimate victory or to bolster his own morale with successes. To do otherwise would be to deliver to him, without contest, the very objectives which he seeks.

Westmoreland's cable made it clear that he intended to hold fast at Khe Sanh. If the North Vietnamese held any thoughts of turning the marine base into another Dien Bien Phu, Westmoreland, it seemed, would relish the opportunity to discourage them. The general's comment to a *Time* correspondent fairly brimmed with confidence. "I hope they try something," he said, "because we are looking for a fight." The unfolding events would oblige him.

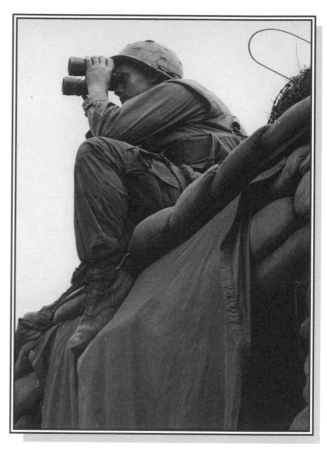

As NVA forces gather near Khe Sanh Combat Base, a marine atop an observation post scans the enemy lines for movement.

CHAPTER TWO

Standing Fast at Khe Sanh: A Place That God Forgot

The opening round in the battle—but not the siege—at Khe Sanh came during the predawn hours of January 2, 1968. Marine sentries in listening post "Dunbar County Lima," located several hundred yards from the west end of the airstrip, reported seeing six men walk past them. An eight-man reaction force led by Lieutenant Nile Buffington, 1st Platoon leader of Lima Company, 3rd Battalion, 26th Marines, responded to the sighting. They arrived moments later at the listening post. Buffington formed his eight marines and the four marines from Dunbar County Lima in single file and prepared for a sweep of the area.

The thirteen marines, each with an M-16 5.56mm rifle on full automatic and magazines containing eighteen rounds, started advancing in the direction where the six intruders had been sighted. By then, a nervous gunner in an army Duster (twin 40mm cannons mounted on an armored tracked vehicle) had opened fire on Buffington's front from Lima Company's right flank.

Suddenly, a 60mm mortar illumination flare, requested by Lima Company commander Captain Richard D. Camp, lit up the night. The flare parachuted gently earthward, its sizzling brilliance turning the plateau into a moonscape of light and shadows. Just as it burned itself out, another popped open to replace it. Then a marine in the center of the file halted abruptly in front of Buffington and the whole line stopped with him. Six figures stood directly ahead of the marines.

Buffington challenged them. After getting no response, he said, "You [deleted] better say something." They answered by firing ten or fifteen rounds at the marines. Buffington felt them whiz past his head. Acting as one, the marines returned fire on full automatic—thirteen marines with 18 rounds for a total of 234 rounds. A heartbeat later, the night fell still.

"Big Fish"

After the marines conducted a brief body search in the dark that turned up nothing, Buffington ordered his troopers back to the company CP (command post). The next morning, Captain Camp returned to the contact area with a search party and "found five dead [of six] NVA officers, all stretched right out on the ground." He later wrote of the previous night's grisly aftermath:

> All of them had been hit from the top of their brain housing groups [heads] to their toenails, and it looked like somebody had raked the ground around them. That was the result of the automatic fire that the listening post fire team and the re-action force had put out. They put out over 230 rounds, and all of them were right on target.

An official marine account of this action maintains that the slain NVA officers were dressed "like Marines." Buffington also recalls that they wore green uniforms. But Camp's recollection of the event differs:

> The dead men were all wearing black pajamas and rubber-soled Ho Chi Minh sandals. All of them were really big men, a lot bigger than most Vietnamese. One of them had pulled a hand grenade halfway out of his pouch, and another one

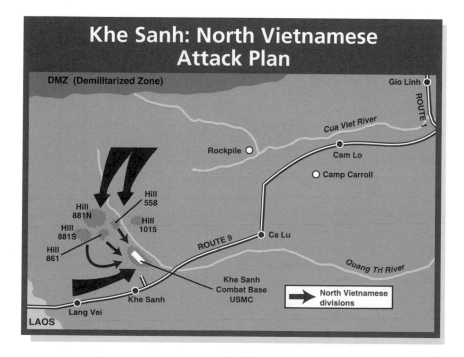

was gripping a pistol with his arm outstretched. Rigor mortis had set in, so they were all frozen in the positions in which they had died, like wax statues.

An intelligence team later examined the enemy remains and determined the five dead men to be high-ranking NVA officers. This revelation did not surprise Camp, who wrote:

> The dead North Vietnamese were definitely big fish; every one of them was wearing a gold or silver belt buckle, not the standard aluminum type. Dispatch cases, pistols, expensive belt buckles—it was obvious to me that those people were special. . . . What it all added up to was that we had killed the commander of an NVA regiment and his staff. . . . The only thing officers as senior as that could have been doing out there was reconnoitering our lines in preparation for a major ground assault.

Operation Niagara

The news of Lima Company's encounter with NVA regimental officers rocketed up the chain of command at jet speed and shook General Westmoreland's MACV headquarters like a sonic boom. The general's long-cherished notion of enticing the enemy into a set-piece battle suddenly appeared to be within his grasp, and the prospect for a showdown excited him. Better yet, rather than having to lure the enemy into a place of American choosing, the enemy was positioning himself right where Westmoreland wanted him.

During the first week of January 1968, the general set in motion the first phase of Operation Niagara—his plan for decisive action at Khe Sanh, aimed at the total destruction of the NVA.

Niagara I, the first phase, called for a far-reaching and exhaustive intelligence-gathering effort to pinpoint enemy positions. Niagara II, the second phase, would then deliver on target the mightiest concentration of aerial firepower and field artillery ever inflicted upon humankind by humankind. Operation Niagara, code-named after the famous American falls, was well calculated "to evoke an image of cascading shells and bombs."

To carry out Niagara II, Westmoreland assembled more than two thousand strategic and tactical aircraft. The wide assortment of aircraft ranged from huge eight-engined B-52 Stratofortress jet bombers down to single-engined A-1 Skyraider prop-driven attack bombers. Some three thousand helicopters added to Niagara's destructive potential. Westmoreland intended to mount a round-the-clock bombardment, while keeping as many as eight hundred aircraft in the air at any given time.

After much bitter interservice bickering for command and control of Niagara II operations, General Westmoreland appointed 7th Air Force commander General William W. Momymer as "single manager for air" at Saigon's Tan Son Nhut airfield. Supplemental air control was to be provided by an aerial computer control center known as Sky Spot, which would coordinate altitudes and speeds of hundreds of aircraft in the crowded skies over Khe Sanh.

Westmoreland ordered the "cascade" on NVA targets to begin on January 21, which coincidentally would mark the beginning of the North Vietnamese bombardment of the Khe Sanh Combat Base.

Girded for Action

General Westmoreland issued no orders to the marines with regard to strengthening defenses at Khe Sanh. He did, however, caution III MAF commander Lieutenant General Robert E. Cushman Jr. (who had relieved Lieutenant General Walt on June 1, 1967) to restrict troop levels to a size capable of being wholly sustained by airlift. This limit would enable the base to operate without need for overland supplies should the Communists seal off the main supply roads at

General Westmoreland (top) assembled a fleet of more than two thousand aircraft in preparation for Operation Niagara. Various strategic and tactical aircraft were brought to Khe Sanh, including the mighty A-1 Skyraider (above) and the B-52 Stratofortress precision bomber (left).

some later date. Acting on the advice of Major General Rathvon Tompkins, commander of the 3rd Marine Division, Cushman sent the 2nd Battalion, 26th Marines, and a third 105mm battery of the 13th Marines into Khe Sanh on January 17. Their airlifted arrival at KSCB marked the first time in over two decades that all units of both outfits had been assembled in one place at one time. They would be needed.

If the new arrivals were expecting the worst at Khe Sanh, they found little there to disappoint them. Chuck Hoover, of 2nd Battalion, 26th Marines, later wrote about his first impressions of the combat base. "I can still recall the day we got to Khe Sanh. It was like a place that God forgot. You knew that death was around." Few of Hoover's comrades would disagree with his perceptions.

The KSCB marines stepped up their defensive preparations, increasing patrol activities and initiating an all-out effort to complete their fortifications. They heaved to, adding trench lines, constructing more sandbagged bunkers, and emplacing extra Claymore mines and stringing triple-coiled barbed wire to their defense perimeter already bristling with German razor tape and speckled with trip flares. Marines holding positions on the several tactically critical hills nearby busied themselves with similar defensive improvements.

Ordnance at KSCB now included six 155mm guns, eighteen 105mm howitzers, eighteen 175mm guns, and four 4.2-inch mortars. Added to these were six M-48 tanks with 90mm guns; ten Ontos tracked antitank vehicles, each fitted with six 106mm

At Khe Sanh Combat Base, marines improved their defenses by building additional sandbagged bunkers (pictured), digging trenches, and securing the base's perimeter with mines and triple-coiled barbed wire.

Electronic Intelligence

Phase I of Operation Niagara—General Westmoreland's plan for a massive bombing and shelling defense of Khe Sanh—centered on developing a detailed intelligence picture of the enemy. The success of Phase II—the full commitment of American airpower and artillery—depended upon an accurate assessment of NVA forces and their locations. Targets had to be identified and pinpointed for destruction. American intelligence analysts drew upon a variety of methods to piece together vital information on enemy movements, including electronic surveillance.

The Americans had dropped hundreds of ACOUSIDS (Acoustic Intrusion Detectors) and ADSIDS (Air-Delivered Seismic Intrusion Detectors) in the jungles around Khe Sanh and along the Ho Chi Minh Trail in nearby Laos.

These remote-controlled, battery-powered devices operated by means of either an acoustic or a seismic sensor. Respectively, the sensors monitored sounds and vibrations of enemy movements.

Little more than a small microphone, the ACOUSID was air-dropped and designed to snag in tree branches, where it would then hang suspended by its parachute. The ADSID, a bomblike canister of electronics, implanted most of its length in the ground upon impact, leaving only an antenna visible.

Both devices were equipped with tiny transmitters that would beep out signals of their collected intelligence data to circling aircraft. Information supplied by these electronic surveillance devices contributed in large measure to the success of Niagara II.

recoilless rifles; and four Duster tracked vehicles with dual-barrel 40mm cannons or quadruple-mounted .50-caliber machine guns. Individual and crew-served weapons—rockets, mortars, light and heavy machine guns—backed up the heavier ordnance. This formidable array excluded supporting artillery from Rockpile and Camp Carroll and the enormous destructive might of American airpower. If the gathering NVA forces were looking for action, they were likely to find it at Khe Sanh. The marines were girded for action.

Increased marine reconnaissance probes in the outlying areas revealed the presence of several new NVA regiments, bivouacked in well-concealed positions partially encircling the combat base. The NVA foot soldiers now enjoyed a substantial numerical edge: two full divisions against three reinforced battalions.

Moreover, U.S. aerial and ground surveillance had totally failed to reveal NVA artillery emplacements across the border in neighboring Laos. Many batteries of 130mm and 152mm guns now stood well within range and zeroed-in on marine targets at Khe Sanh. Closer yet, hidden in the dense jungle foliage, the NVA had installed an imposing assortment of lighter artillery and

122mm and 140mm rockets. Lastly, to defend this impressive array of weaponry against air attack, the North Vietnamese had positioned great numbers of 37mm automatic antiaircraft cannons and .51-caliber antiaircraft machine guns.

The marines were not the only ones girded for action.

Little to Lose

On January 18, a patrol from Captain William H. Dabney's India Company engaged an NVA force in a firefight on the supposedly unoccupied slopes of Hill 881 North. The next day, another India Company patrol grappled with the enemy in a similar encounter on 881N. The enemy was obviously up to something. Captain Dabney, responsible for maintaining an outpost on Hill 881 South, wanted to find out what. He requested and got permission from 3rd Battalion commander Colonel Harry Alderman to conduct a company-size reconnaissance on 881N. Alderman dispatched most of Mike Company, the battalion reserve, to cover Dabney's outpost.

On January 20, Dabney led his India Company marines through a thick early morning fog toward the base of 881N. They met no resistance until they started up the steep slopes in the late morning. The fog had lifted by then, exposing the marines in open terrain. Suddenly, a thunderous hail of automatic-weapons fire and rocket-propelled grenades poured down upon them from an unseen enemy above. The rain of fire chopped down twenty marines in less than sixty seconds, leaving them wounded and out of action.

Dabney radioed for heavy fire support. Within minutes, ninety-five-pound 155mm shells started whooshing past the pinned-down marines and began pulverizing enemy positions on the high ground. The marines advanced slowly upward. After more than five hours of pitched battle with the NVA, India Company gained a point just below the summit. The gain was bought with the blood of four dead and forty wounded marines. Dabney called for reinforcements.

With India Company in position to overrun Hill 881 North, Colonel Lownds denied Dabney's request and ordered India Company back to its outpost positions on Hill 881 South. Neither Dabney nor his marines could believe the base commander's order. But the colonel had acted with good reason in directing India Company's withdrawal to the relative safety of its hilltop outpost.

At 1400 that afternoon, Lieutenant La Thanh Tonc, a North Vietnamese artillery officer, had surrendered to Bravo Company, 1st Battalion, 26th Marines, at the airstrip's west end. Incredibly, Tonc, seeking asylum, was willing to tell his captors the whole NVA plan of attack, set to commence shortly after midnight that very night. The first assaults would target Hills 881 South and

Captain of Fate

The North Vietnamese Army launched its initial assault on the Khe Sanh Combat Base shortly after midnight on January 21, 1968. Was it by some quirk of fate that the NVA bypassed Hill 881 South that night? Or was it because of India Company's scrappy marines? India Company commander Captain William H. Dabney felt sure that earlier aggressive actions by his marines had done much to discourage an enemy attack on 881S:

> Hill 881S was the only outlying Khe Sanh Combat Base position not assaulted by infantry on the night of January 20–21. . . . Hill 861 got hit, the Khe Sanh ville [village] got hit. Everything I heard about around there got hit that night, except 881S, and we were the most exposed. I

was convinced . . . that we were not assaulted only because we'd been patrolling aggressively for a month out to the limit of our prudence and had developed our own intelligence as a result of those patrols and had acted on it within the limits of our capabilities. I believe that the India Company recon-in-force [large reconnaissance force] to 881N on January 20 ran into the NVA battalion that was designated to attack us that night. We could not destroy it, but we found and fixed it in the subsequent fire fight and hit it with supporting arms. Although it may not have decimated the battalion, it probably discouraged it.

Some might say that under Dabney's inspired leadership, India Company captained its own fate.

861, followed by a major thrust on the main base. The NVA intended to crush the marines at Khe Sanh and then sweep eastward to overrun the cities of Quang Tri and Hue.

Marine commanders decided that they had little to lose by believing Tonc—and rightfully so. Tonc had told the truth.

No Dinbinphoo!

On January 21, General Westmoreland assessed the situation at Khe Sanh. Late that afternoon, he sent a cable expressing his findings to Joint Chiefs of Staff chairman Wheeler and Admiral U. S. Grant Sharp, the Commander in Chief, Pacific. Convinced of the imminence of a major NVA effort in either Quang Tri or Thua Thien, Westmoreland wrote of his enemy:

> He has made determined attempts to gain a spectacular victory, and is now preparing for another attempt in northern First Corps. I believe that the enemy sees a similarity between our base at Khe Sanh and Dien Bien Phu and hopes, by following a pattern of activity similar to that used against the French, to gain similar military and political ends.

The Khe Sanh Shuffle

Marines at Khe Sanh soon learned that survival depended on quick reaction to the first sound of incoming mortar, rocket, or artillery fire. They developed an almost instinctive technique of running and diving for cover at a split second's notice. In a sense, their movements constituted a kind of bizarre dance with death. They began to call it the Khe Sanh shuffle.

On January 24, India Company's gunnery sergeant DeArmond called company commander Bill Dabney's attention to the "music of the dance" for the first time on Hill 881 South. Dabney recalls:

> I'd never had artillery fired at me, so I didn't really know what to keep listening for; but he had been at the Chosin Reservoir and in the big fighting in Korea, so [the gunny] had some experience with it.

I listened more closely and after a while, during these rocket salvos, more or less coincident with them, if you listened very closely you could hear way, way out, to the west, a kind of pop, boom, that sort of thing, and . . . if you listened fifteen, twenty seconds later, over the hill, you'd hear this . . . like a squirrel running through dry leaves.

> Well, we reported it . . . down to Khe Sanh by radio. The response we got back initially [because it was the first use of heavy artillery against the Americans] was, "Oh, they don't have any heavy artillery out there."

The reply of disbelief from Khe Sanh did not deter the marines on Hill 881 South from practicing the Khe Sanh shuffle.

Shortly thereafter, Westmoreland declared the situation at Khe Sanh to be critical, to the extent that it might represent the turning point of the Vietnam War. In Washington, President Lyndon Baines Johnson received the news with anger, frustration, and grave concern.

President Johnson (left) listens intently as one of his generals discusses the military situation in Vietnam.

America's commitment in Vietnam began under President Dwight D. Eisenhower and extended in time through the presidencies of John F. Kennedy, Lyndon B. Johnson, Richard M. Nixon, and Gerald R. Ford. Despite the succession of U.S. presidents who held office during that tragic period in the history of both nations, the Vietnam War will be remembered by most Americans as LBJ's war.

A major setback in the war might send a signal to the American people that an American defeat in Vietnam was inevitable. Already torn by the increasing antiwar sentiment in the United States, Johnson did not want to be remembered as the president who lost the war in Vietnam. When news of the North Vietnamese attack on Hill 861 reached him, he reacted sharply to his advisers. "I don't want any damn Dinbinphoo [Dien Bien Phu]!" he rasped.

"Situation at Khe Sanh"

Westmoreland reacted quickly to the enemy threat at Khe Sanh, ordering the immediate start of Niagara II on January 21. The next day, Lieutenant Colonel John F. Mitchell's 1st Battalion, 9th Marines, was rushed into the besieged base by helicopter from Camp Evans in the Hue/Phu Bai area. Khe Sanh received its last major reinforcement on January 27, when Captain Hoang Pho's 37th ARVN Ranger Battalion arrived from Phu Loc. The defenders at the combat base and in the surrounding hills now numbered 6,680.

ARVN rangers maintain posts in a trench along the perimeter of Khe Sanh Combat Base. Additional American and South Vietnamese troops were brought to Khe Sanh to protect against the mounting NVA threat.

The NVA kept blasting away at the base with artillery fire, rockets, and mortars every day for the rest of the month. But the anticipated all-out ground assault failed to come when expected.

In Washington, President Johnson monitored the activities at Khe Sanh on a daily basis in the White House Situation Room. He became obsessed with the need for averting another "Dinbinphoo." To help ease his mind, two of the president's most trusted advisers asked General Wheeler for a written assurance from the Joint Chiefs that Khe Sanh would be defended at all costs. The general complied on January 29, issuing a memorandum entitled "The Situation at Khe Sanh" (JCSM-63-68).

Far from a spirited battle cry, the JCS memorandum (signed only by Wheeler "for" the Joint Chiefs) simply declared that "the Joint Chiefs of Staff have reviewed the situation at Khe Sanh and concur with General Westmoreland's assessment. . . . They recommend that we maintain our position at Khe Sanh." This mildly worded statement probably did little to bolster the president's confidence in the Joint Chiefs' resolve to stand fast at Khe Sanh.

Only hours after Wheeler issued his statement, fast-breaking events elsewhere in Vietnam dramatically diverted the president's attention from the "situation at Khe Sanh."

CHAPTER THREE

Tet: Blood in the Streets

On the eve of the Tet holidays, the headquarters of the National Liberation Front issued a general order to its members. The order began with a poem marking the start of the Year of the Monkey, written especially for the occasion by Ho Chi Minh.

> This Spring far outshines the
> previous Springs,
> Of victories throughout the land
> come happy tidings.
> Let North and South emulate each
> other in fighting the U.S.
> aggressors!
> Forward!
> Total Victory will be ours.

Ho's poem, which was also broadcast by Radio Hanoi, was followed by an explanation for the forthcoming assaults on South Vietnamese and American installations. The Tet attacks were designed to "restore power to the people, liberate the people of the South, and fulfill our revolutionary task of establishing democracy throughout the country." The order continued: "This will be the greatest battle ever fought in the history of this country. It will bring forth worldwide changes, but will also require many sacrifices." The battle that would, like a lightning flash, "split the sky and shake the earth" began at 0135 on January 30—a full day early.

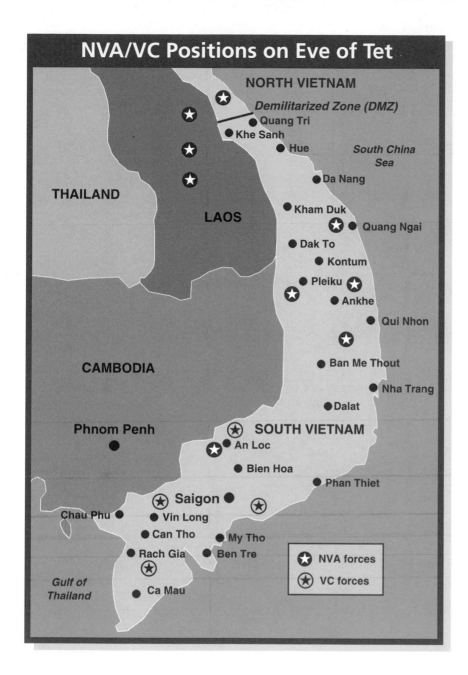

NVA/VC Positions on Eve of Tet

NORTH VIETNAM

Demilitarized Zone (DMZ)

Quang Tri

Khe Sanh

Hue

South China Sea

Da Nang

Kham Duk

Quang Ngai

Dak To

Kontum

Pleiku

Ankhe

Qui Nhon

Ban Me Thout

Nha Trang

Dalat

THAILAND

LAOS

CAMBODIA

Phnom Penh

SOUTH VIETNAM

An Loc

Bien Hoa

Phan Thiet

Chau Phu

Saigon

Vin Long

Can Tho

My Tho

Rach Gia

Ben Tre

Gulf of Thailand

Ca Mau

NVA forces

VC forces

Westmoreland's Wait

A day before the start of the lunar holidays, whether by design or accident, NVA/VC forces launched attacks on government buildings and military posts in Nha Trang, Ban Me Thuot, Kontum, Hoi Nan, Da Nang, Qui Nhon, and Pleiku. They struck with mortars, rockets, and small-arms fire. The long-rumored Communist attack, it seemed, had begun at last.

Although long expected, the enemy assaults achieved total tactical (as opposed to strategic) surprise. Westmoreland, of course, had dismissed the possibility of attack *during* the Tet

Although he was alerted to the immediate threat at Khe Sanh, South Vietnamese president Nguyen Van Thieu proceeded with celebrations of the upcoming Tet holiday.

holidays. Despite his regard for history, the general seemingly paid no heed to the timing of a legendary event in Vietnam's past: Emperor Quang Trung succeeded in driving the hated Chinese from Vietnam by launching a surprise attack on the Chinese garrison at Hanoi—during Tet 1789. Interestingly, a statuette of the great Vietnamese hero stood in Westmoreland's Saigon villa, a silent reminder of an earlier Tet offensive.

At the start of Tet 1968, General Westmoreland ordered all U.S. forces in the south to full alert and warned President Nguyen Van Thieu of the immediate danger. Thieu agreed to reduce the Tet cease-fire to thirty-six hours and cancel half—but not all—ARVN leaves. To cancel *all* leaves, he feared, would cause ARVN morale to suffer needlessly. Thieu neglected to say just how he intended to recall his scattered forces from holiday festivities and return them to their barracks in a timely fashion. The president himself left Saigon to spend Tet with his wife's family in nearby My Tho. It would seem that he failed to grasp the seriousness of the situation.

The first attacks, launched a day early, proved to be far less effective and much more easily countered than Westmoreland had expected. Most of the attackers had been driven off, rounded up, or killed by late in the day on January 30. What appeared to be the vaunted enemy offensive had been contained fairly easily. Many Americans and South Vietnamese breathed a sigh of relief and adopted a false sense of security. Brigadier General Phillip B. Davidson, chief of MACV intelligence, was not among them.

Davidson had spent the early morning hours of January 30 at MACV headquarters at Tan Son Nhut air base outside Saigon. After carefully monitoring and analyzing reports of the fighting in the north, he sensed that the worst was still to come. "This is going to happen in the rest of the country tonight or tomorrow morning," he warned General Westmoreland.

Westmoreland agreed, but he could do little to improve his defenses. Half of his combat troops were concentrated in the I Corps sector, the far northern provinces defended by the marines. The other half were already spread thin across the II, III, and IV Corps sectors that stretched from the two northernmost provinces to the Mekong Delta. Westmoreland was forced to rely on Thieu's ARVN forces to defend the cities and towns most subject to attack. And half of the ARVN soldiers were still on leave.

As the MACV commander faced perhaps the greatest battle of his long and dedicated career, he could only stand and wait.

The Real Thing

The full force and fury of Giap's "General Offensive, General Uprising" erupted like a long-dormant volcano one night, beginning on January 30 and ending on the 31st. Violent explosions echoed across the land. Streams of NVA and Vietcong marauders swept through the cities, towns, and villages of South Vietnam like bubbling lava floes, spreading death and destruction in their path. Notwithstanding Westmoreland's alert orders and despite American warnings that a second wave of attacks would commence that very night, the second-round assaults also achieved absolute tactical surprise.

The scale of the operations boggled the mind and defied the imagination. More than eighty-four thousand Communist fighters arose almost ghostlike from apparently nowhere to attack 36 of 44 provincial capitals, 5 of 6 autonomous cities, 64 of 242 district capitals, and 23 airfields or bases.

In I Corps, strong Communist forces penetrated defenses at Quang Tri, Tam Ky, and Hue. At Phu Bai and Chu Lai, U.S. military installations withstood additional enemy attacks in strength. In II Corps, the Communists assaulted Tuy Hoa, Phan Thiet, and the American bases at Bong Son and An Khe. In III Corps, offensive thrusts were directed at key targets within the Capital Military Zone of Saigon and adjacent Gia Dinh Province. The ARVN headquarters at Bien Hoa and the U.S. II Field Force headquarters at Long Binh also experienced major assaults. In IV Corps, defended primarily by ARVN troops, the fighting grew especially savage, as the Communists struck hard at Vinh Long, My Tho, Can Tho, and Ben Tre. Almost every other provincial and district capital in the Mekong Delta came under Communist attack.

Brigadier General John R. Chaisson, III MAF operations staff officer, later described the explosive Communist onslaught as "surprisingly well-coordinated, surprisingly intensive, and launched with a surprising amount of audacity." Indeed, if the attacks of the previous night had left any question as to the start of the Tet Offensive, the Communist resurgence of January 30 and 31 provided the answer. This was the real thing.

Children run past rubble and damaged cars in Saigon, trying to escape fighting between South Vietnamese and NVA forces.

The Battle for Saigon

Shortly after 0300 on January 31, marine guards awakened Ellsworth Bunker, the U.S. ambassador in Saigon. "Saigon is under attack," they declared. Four blocks away, nineteen members of the Vietcong C-10 Sapper

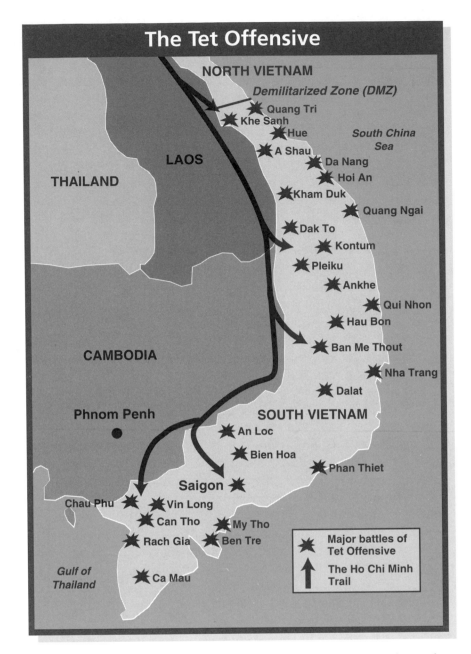

The Tet Offensive

NORTH VIETNAM

Demilitarized Zone (DMZ)

Quang Tri

Khe Sanh

Hue

South China Sea

A Shau

Da Nang

Hoi An

Kham Duk

Quang Ngai

Dak To

Kontum

Pleiku

Ankhe

Qui Nhon

Hau Bon

Ban Me Thout

Nha Trang

Dalat

SOUTH VIETNAM

An Loc

Bien Hoa

Phan Thiet

Saigon

Chau Phu

Vin Long

Can Tho

My Tho

Rach Gia

Ben Tre

Ca Mau

Gulf of Thailand

CAMBODIA

Phnom Penh

THAILAND

LAOS

Major battles of Tet Offensive

The Ho Chi Minh Trail

Battalion (special assault/demolition forces) were assaulting the American Embassy. The marines, expecting an attack on the ambassador's residence at any moment, hustled Bunker into an armored personnel carrier and whisked him away to the home of the chief of embassy security. They thought he might be safer there. But safety was a very relative asset right then in the South Vietnamese capital.

The true start of the Tet Offensive exploded in the streets of Saigon at 0130. Thirteen men and one woman of the elite C-10 Sapper Battalion, all native Saigonese, stormed the staff entrance of Independence Palace on Nguyen Du Street. They shouted, "Open the palace gates! We are the Liberation Army!" then blasted away at the gate with B-40 rockets.

Automatic-weapons fire greeted their attempt to crash into the palace, forcing the sappers to seek cover in an unfinished apartment building across the street. Two U.S. MPs rushed to the building with M-60 machine guns and were gunned down in the running gun battle that followed. The battle lasted two days, as ARVN troops, American MPs, and the National Police tried to dislodge the sappers. Throughout the two-day siege, American TV cameras recorded the action for viewers of the six o'clock news back home. In the end, all of the sappers were either killed or captured.

Additional elements of the C-10 Sapper Battalion, which consisted of some 250 men and women, spearheaded the Communist assault on the city. They were assigned to take and hold the presidential palace, the American Embassy, and the national radio station, as well as several other key targets.

About five thousand local force (Vietcong) troops—thirty-five battalions in all—commanded by North Vietnamese General Tran Do followed the lead of the sappers. Most of Tran's troops had infiltrated the city in the days just prior to Tet. They attacked from the north, the west, and the south, in a three-pronged thrust toward the center of Saigon. The attack within the city was aimed at crippling the ability of U.S. and ARVN forces to react effectively by seizing key government and military facilities.

Simultaneously, in the outlying areas of Saigon, encircling Communist forces moved to disrupt allied lines of communications and neutralize potential U.S.

(Below) Clouds of smoke hover over the streets of Saigon following the Communist attack on the South Vietnamese capital. (Below, left) Meanwhile, U.S. soldiers plow through the ruins of Saigon, flushing out Vietcong guerrillas.

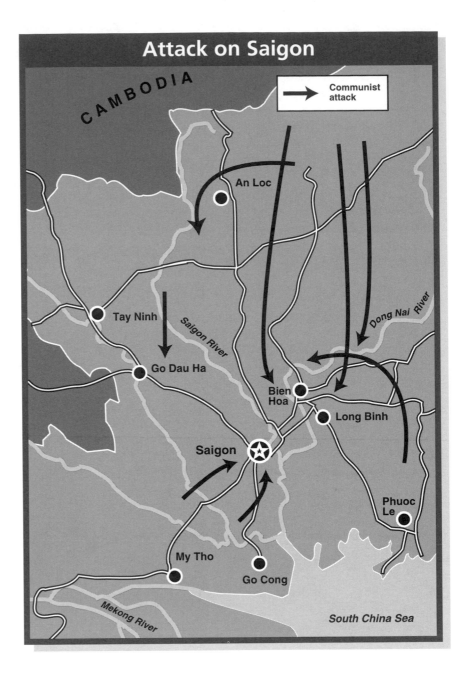

Attack on Saigon

CAMBODIA

An Loc

Communist attack

Tay Ninh

Saigon River

Dong Nai River

Go Dau Ha

Bien Hoa

Long Binh

Saigon

Phuoc Le

My Tho

Go Cong

Mekong River

South China Sea

and South Vietnamese reinforcements. The VC 5th Division struck the huge U.S. and ARVN bases at Long Binh and Bien Hoa. At the old Michelin plantation at Lai Khe, the NVA 7th Division assaulted the U.S. 1st Infantry Division and ARVN 5th Division headquarters. And at Cu Chi, the VC 9th Division hammered the headquarters of the U.S. 25th Infantry Division.

All told, these combined attacks involved all of the Capital Military Zone and much of the III Corps Military Tactical Zone. But world attention centered on the battle for Saigon, for, in full view of the television cameras, the credibility of America's vaunted military might was undergoing its strongest test ever.

Newspapers and television networks brought the embassy battle home to Americans with startling prose, vivid photography, and a prophecy of doom. Embassy scenes of bullet-riddled walls, of American MPs lying facedown in death where they had fallen, and of the bloody corpses of slain Vietcong scattered about the embassy lawns were displayed again and again on television and in newspapers and magazines across America. Media coverage of the Tet Offensive in the winter of 1968 succeeded as never before in shocking the conscience of America and adding to its discontent about the war.

A Pattern of Defeat

Actually, the quickly repulsed break-in at the U.S. Embassy compound represented what was probably the smallest action of the overall assault on Saigon. By day's end, American and ARVN troops had turned away similar attacks on principal political targets at Independence Palace, the South Vietnamese Joint General Staff headquarters, Armored Command headquarters, Artillery Command headquarters, and navy headquarters. Frances FitzGerald, an acclaimed American journalist who has lived in Vietnam, later described the fighting of January 31 in Saigon:

American MPs collect weapons and gather the dead in the aftermath of the attack on the U.S. Embassy.

> Forced to fight on their own terrain, the American and GVN [government of South Vietnam] commanders committed tanks, helicopter gunships, and bombers to the counteroffensive. By the end of the day they had burned the radio station to the ground, and bombed into ruins the model cotton mill outside the city and the single low-income project ever built by the municipality. But the NLF [Vietcong] were not so easily dislodged. Holing up in Cholon [a Chinese suburb] and around the Phu Tho racetrack, they held out for two weeks, alternately disappearing and reappearing to direct sniper fire against the ARVN troops. The city was in chaos.

Meanwhile, at nearby Tan Son Nhut air base and the adjacent MACV compound, 3rd Armored Squadron troops of the U.S. 25th Infantry Division and elements of the 8th ARVN Airborne Battalion fought off more than seven hundred VC attackers.

President Thieu declared a state of martial law in Saigon on January 31. But General Westmoreland exuded confidence at a press conference the next day. Noting that fifty-eight hundred Communists had already been killed, the general predicted that the enemy offensive "is about to run out of steam."

The Shot Seen Round the World

One of the most disturbing examples of the power of the press and television to control public opinion came out of a shooting incident in the streets of Saigon. On the morning of January 31, Eddie Adams, an Associated Press photographer, and Vo Suu, a Vietnamese TV cameraman working for the National Broadcasting Company, had been cruising the embattled city looking for camera-worthy subjects. Near the An Quang temple, they found one. A slight man with hands tied behind his back was being led up the street by South Vietnamese marines.

Although the man wore no military uniform or insignia, a reporter on the scene identified the captive to Adams and Suu as a Vietcong officer. Dressed in a short-sleeved plaid shirt, black pants, and sandals, the prisoner showed signs of having been beaten. In full view of clicking and whirring cameras, the marines halted the alleged VC in front of General Nguyen Ngoc Loan, chief of South Vietnam's National Police.

Loan drew his pistol and started waving away onlookers. He then turned abruptly, extended his spindly right arm, and, with shocking suddenness, shot the prisoner in the head. The victim grimaced, Loan's pistol smoked, and the cameras captured the violence for all eternity. More than twenty million Americans watched the fifty-two-second TV sequence. And Adams won the Pulitzer Prize for his photograph, which has since appeared untold hundreds of times in books, magazines, and newspapers.

In its zeal to report the more gory aspects of a complicated war in a complex time, however, the media rarely attempted to make clear the details behind this seemingly brutal execution. The executed man was in fact a Vietcong officer who had just killed a police major—one of Loan's best friends—and knifed the major's entire family. Moreover, under the rules of war, military personnel caught not wearing a uniform or identifying insignia in a war zone are subject to being executed as spies.

General Nguyen Ngoc Loan executes a Vietcong officer, who grimaces at the impact of the fatal bullet.

Although fighting in the Saigon area grew intense in early February, American and ARVN forces quickly squelched all major enemy efforts. By February 7, American and ARVN forces had cleared the city of all but small, isolated enemy units. House-to-house fighting with the Communists continued, until allied troops regained control of the suburbs on February 23. During this period, the enemy was twice more repulsed at Tan Son Nhut.

A pattern quickly emerged in the tumult that was Tet, as American and ARVN forces, superior in both firepower and numbers, defeated the NVA and VC attackers in individual battles across the land. Most encounters lasted less than a week. Tet's bitterest and bloodiest battle was fought in the streets of Hue.

In Tan Son Nhut, the bodies of American soldiers who were killed during the fierce fighting between allied and NVA/VC forces are piled onto an armored personnel carrier.

CHAPTER FOUR

New City: A Moving Experience

During the first dark hours of January 31, 1968, marine trucks loaded with wounded, sixteen vehicles in all, drew heavy fire on the way to the medevac helicopter landing zone near the U.S. Military Assistance Command, Vietnam (MACV) compound in Hue. The marines sustained four more seriously wounded by the time they reached the LZ on the Perfume River.

Soon, the sound of *whup-whup-whupping* chopper blades announced the medevac's arrival, unseen in the pitch black and foggy nighttime sky. Corporal Chisler, a tall black marine from 1st Battalion, 1st Marines, got on the radio, braved enemy fire, and guided the chopper down through the murk to a perfect landing at his feet.

The medevac pilot peered into the dark and said, "Where are you. I can't see." Chisler banged on the nose of the chopper.

The pilot wanted a casualty count.

"Twenty, sir," Chisler said.

"You only called with sixteen."

"Yes, sir," Chisler acknowledged, "but a funny thing happened on the [way] to the landing zone." He paused, then said, "We know you can make it."

They loaded the casualties aboard the helicopter, a Sea Knight. One of the wounded, Army Specialist Fourth Class Frank Dozerman, died on the flight to the hospital. It was the end of the first day's fighting for Hue. One down, twenty-four days to go.

The End of Restraint

The ancient city of Hue—the old imperial capital of Vietnam—stands halfway between Da Nang and the DMZ separating the two Vietnams. Hue (pronounced Way), with an estimated population of 140,000, plus uncounted thousands of refugees, was South Vietnam's third largest city in 1968. Sliced in two by the Huong Giang, or River of Perfumes, two-thirds of the population lived within the walls of the Old City, or Citadel, north of the river.

Modeled after the Imperial City at Beijing, the Citadel is a roughly square fortress, surrounded by sixteen-foot-high walls about two miles long on the sides and ranging in thickness from sixty to more than two hundred feet. Moats or canals trace three exterior sides of the fortress city, while the fourth side borders the river in the south. The Imperial Palace, where Annamese royalty once held court, stands contained within the square, in company with many other ancient and revered structures.

The more Westernized, basically residential New City lies south of the river, tied to the Imperial City by the Nguyen Hoang Bridge. Shaped roughly like a triangle, the newer city's north side borders the Perfume River. The slender Phu Cam Canal flows down from the wider Perfume River, then turns back up, forming a V of sorts around the city's south side.

Beyond Hue, the Perfume River meanders eastward and flows into the South China Sea some five miles distant. Although too shallow to accommodate deep-water vessels, the river normally bustles with local water traffic. Navy supply boats found it useful for hauling supplies upriver from Da Nang to Hue during the Vietnam War.

Throughout most of the war, both sides regarded Hue almost as an open city. Except for an ARVN reaction company of special troops called Black Panthers, only U.S. and South Vietnamese staff and garrison troops were stationed in Hue.

The Citadel housed the headquarters of Brigadier General Ngo Quang Truong's 1st ARVN Division. Across the river, the Hue Ramp Detachment, U.S. Naval Support Activity, operated a U.S. Navy boat ramp in New City. And in a compound several hundred yards down Route 1 from the ramp, soldiers of the U.S. MACV lived and worked comfortably in a cluster of two- and three-story buildings.

Despite the city's obvious military value, the Vietcong, until now, had excluded Hue from their terrorist activities. Their restraint ended abruptly in the predawn hours of January 31, 1968—the second day of the Tet Offensive.

A gateway stands within the ancient Citadel of Hue. Vietcong marauders attacked the imperial fortress on January 31, 1968.

A Call for Help

Two regiments of regular NVAs that had infiltrated Hue in early January shed their civilian clothes and commenced attacking the city from within. Their attack was timed to coincide with an NVA mortar and rocket barrage from without. Two infantry battalions of the 6th NVA Regiment and the 12th Sapper Battalion advanced on the 1st ARVN Division headquarters from the southwest.

The Communists appeared to have two main objectives—the 1st ARVN Division headquarters in the Citadel and the MACV compound in the southern section of the city. In the end, they would fail to achieve either objective.

The Black Panthers stopped the NVA 800th Battalion briefly at the Hue airstrip but were soon forced to withdraw to ARVN headquarters (HQ). Except for the ARVN HQ, the entire Citadel fell to the NVA 6th Regiment by daybreak.

North of the city, the NVA 806th Battalion moved into blocking positions to cut off potential attempts to reinforce the Hue defenders.

In New City, the NVA 4th Regiment assaulted the MACV compound and was twice repulsed. Two Vietcong battalions seized control of all other government buildings, as the NVA 810th Battalion positioned itself to block reinforcement attempts from the south.

Meanwhile, General Ngo Quang Truong had ordered his 3rd Regiment, reinforced by two airborne battalions and an armored cavalry troop, to fight its way into the city from positions along Route 1. They reached his headquarters late in the day on January 31. Truong ordered a counterattack the next morning.

Marines take cover behind a tank as sniper fire breaks out in the streets of Hue. In a matter of a few hours, the Communist forces had captured nearly the entire Citadel.

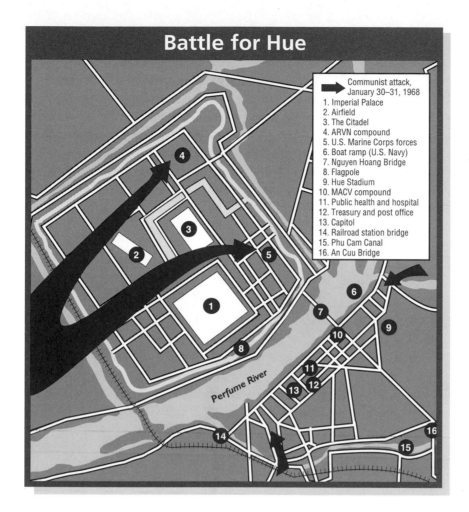

Battle for Hue

Communist attack, January 30–31, 1968

1. Imperial Palace
2. Airfield
3. The Citadel
4. ARVN compound
5. U.S. Marine Corps forces
6. Boat ramp (U.S. Navy)
7. Nguyen Hoang Bridge
8. Flagpole
9. Hue Stadium
10. MACV compound
11. Public health and hospital
12. Treasury and post office
13. Capitol
14. Railroad station bridge
15. Phu Cam Canal
16. An Cuu Bridge

Perfume River

With Truong's troops occupied, the South Vietnamese general responsible for the entire northern combat zone asked U.S. forces to take full charge of clearing Hue south of the Perfume River. By then, U.S. Marines were already working to accommodate him.

Street Without Joy

Reports of the attack on Hue poured into the closest marine base at Phu Bai during the early morning hours of January 31. Phu Bai, twelve clicks (kilometers) southwest of Hue, was the home of Task Force X-Ray, commanded by Brigadier General Foster C. Lahue. Lahue's task force had been established on January 13 and assigned to protect the large tactical area of responsibility (TAOR) that extended from south of Da Nang to slightly north of Hue. The mission of the task force included defending the base at Phu Bai, screening the western approaches to Hue, and keeping Route 1 open between Hai Van Pass and Hue.

This mission and TAOR represented a huge undertaking for Task Force X-Ray, which consisted of only three understaffed battalions—

Stationed at the marine base at Phu Bai, Brigadier General Foster C. Lahue and his Task Force X-Ray were responsible for protecting the tactical area that stretched from Da Nang to Hue.

a scant four thousand troops. Two full regiments, totaling three times that number, would normally be allocated for such a sizable task. With his task force spread thinly in the field and itself already taking NVA mortar fire, Brigadier General Lahue could hardly spare troops to help out at Hue. But orders came down from III MAF headquarters to send reinforcements to Hue. Lahue had to do *something*. He elected to send Alpha Company, 1st Battalion, 1st Marines—the only company readily available.

Much of the credit for Alpha Company's well-deserved reputation as an excellent fighting outfit belonged to its commander, Captain Gordon D. Batcheller. Twenty-eight years old, the strapping, keen-minded, former Princeton football star had been appointed Alpha's company commander on Christmas Day, 1967. Batcheller, a born leader, called his appointment "the all-time great Christmas present." His troopers loved and respected him.

One Alpha lance corporal recalled, "Captain Batcheller was a big dude who was always up front when the [deleted] hit the fan."

Batcheller got the word before dawn on January 30 to "saddle up" Alpha Company and stand by to move out. His company, like the entire task force, was seriously understrength. He could assemble only two and a half platoons—about 110 marines. At first light, the Alpha Company relief force boarded trucks and headed up Route 1, the road called the Street Without Joy because so many Frenchmen had met death on it in years past.

Blood and Blue Sky

En route to Hue, Alpha Company chanced upon a group of four M-48 tanks belonging to the 3rd Tank Battalion of the 3rd Marine Division. The tankers, led by Lieutenant Colonel Edward J. LaMontagne, joined the rifle company and together they continued on toward Hue. They hoped to link up with the embattled MACV compound inside New City. Just south of the city, they crossed over the Phu Cam Canal on the An Cuu Bridge, with the M-48s out in front. Batcheller called a halt across the canal and ordered his troops to board the tanks. On his command, the tanks roared off into the outskirts of New City, with all hands firing into the wooden buildings to cover their approach.

Well-hidden NVA troops returned fire immediately. Out of nowhere, a B-40 rocket smashed into Batcheller's lead tank and exploded. The tank shook and shuddered. Another explosion. The concussion ruptured Batcheller's eardrum. Shrapnel sliced him with minor wounds. A spray of AK-47 automatic fire raked across the street in front of the advancing marines. Marines started dropping all over the place. They took cover in a ditch, dragging their wounded out of harm's way. The NVAs kept firing. Mortar rounds exploded here and there. The marines answered back, *pop-pop-popping* away with their M-16s.

Batcheller and LaMontagne brought their big guns to bear. The M-48s opened up with their booming 90mm cannons. Gunners on truck-mounted quad-fifties poured streams of steel on anything resembling a target. The tanks advanced slowly, but the MACV compound still lay a long way ahead of them, across an open field of rice paddies. And the NVA fire showed no signs of letting up.

After killing the NVA soldiers in two large buildings, a column of marines attempted to move past Batcheller's tank, but an NVA machine gun cut down on them. A navy man with the column took a hit and went down. The others scattered. Batcheller moved forward to drag the wounded man to safety behind the tank but was himself raked with machine-gun fire. Bullets ripped gaping holes in his right forearm, right thigh, and left knee. The impact of the high-velocity rounds tossed him in the air and flipped his body into a roll of concertina (barbed wire) on the side of the leaf-covered road. Blood covered his fatigues and flak jacket. He warned his marines to stay back.

Convinced that he would bleed to death, Batcheller stared up at a bright blue sky and prepared himself for death.

Questionable Orders

News of Alpha Company's plight reached Phu Bai at about noon on January 31. Brigadier General Lahue, now even hard-pressed to muster additional relief forces, summoned Lieutenant Colonel Marcus J. Gravel, commander of the 1st Battalion, 1st Marines. At Lahue's direction, Gravel hastily organized another reaction force. This second relief force consisted of Gravel's own command group, including himself and his operations officer, Major Walter M. Murphy; Golf Company, on loan from the 2nd Battalion, 5th Marines; a tank platoon; and a handful of engineers.

While this makeshift group was assembling, Lieutenant Richard Lyons, USN, a Catholic chaplain, returned to camp by helicopter, back from visiting some battalion wounded in Da Nang. Gravel wheeled up to the helipad in a jeep and hailed Lyons. "Do you want to go into Hue City for an afternoon of street fighting?" The chaplain, who had been known on occasion to fire off a few covering rounds during medevac operations, welcomed the chance to string along. Lyons hopped into the jeep and Gravel tore off to join Golf Company at the battalion assembly area.

Gravel's instructions to his assembled troops were brief. "Get on the trucks!" he commanded. At 1230, his combined force headed up the joyless street toward Hue.

When they crossed the An Cuu Bridge, Gravel's truck convoy, which included a couple of Dusters with 40mm guns, ran into a road jam of stalled tanks, trucks, and troops. Just up the road, Alpha Company was still pinned down but holding in place. Gravel moved up to join Alpha. His troops gathered up

Semper Fidelis

Master Gunnery Sergeant Jenaro Lucero, the operations chief of the 1st Marine Regiment, exemplified what being a marine is all about. Lucero, a large man with a menacing mustache, was working on his third tour of duty in Vietnam when interviewed in the MACV compound in February 1968. Asked why he elected to spend so much time in Vietnam, he answered, "This is it, it's where a Marine belongs. It's what I have been trained to do all my life. I am just paying back the investment the Marine Corps has made in me."

In answer to what he thought about the fighting in Hue, Lucero said, "The Marine Corps is kicking the NVA where it hurts the most. It's only a matter of days now before he is done for." The top sergeant, who served as an automatic rifleman with the 5th Marines in Korea, added, "These young Marines fighting in the city are better equipped and better trained than the NVA. Oh, the NVA is a good trooper, make no mistake, he's damn good, but he still doesn't hold a candle to any Marine. Besides that, he's up against the two best regiments in the Corps, the 1st and the 5th."

Alpha's wounded, including Captain Batcheller, and sent them back to Phu Bai on one truck, unescorted. This crude evacuation was risky business, to be sure, but better than letting wounded marines die in the field.

Golf Company, under Captain Charles Meadows, moved forward of the depleted Alpha Company, and Gravel's armored convoy of marines fought on through the NVA resistance. They arrived at the battered MACV compound in New City at 1430.

Major Wayne R. Swenson, the Task Force X-Ray liaison officer to the 1st ARVN Division, said later, "I have little doubt that many of us [at the compound] would not be alive today, had those Marines not arrived."

By then, marine casualties totaled ten dead and another forty wounded. Gravel would need replacements before he could mount an effective clearing operation in New City. But often in combat situations there is no time for needed things. Right then, as it turned out, was one of those times.

At that point, the X-Ray command staff at Phu Bai radioed orders to Lieutenant Colonel Gravel from General Lahue. The orders, which had originated at III MAF in Da Nang, instructed Gravel to advance across the Perfume River with Alpha and Golf Companies and hook up with General Truong's besieged ARVN headquarters in the Citadel. Gravel shook his head in disbelief. It became painfully clear to him that the high command did not understand the situation at Hue.

In the chaos and confusion of the Tet attacks, sullied intelligence, and disrupted lines of communication, the top-level commanders at Da Nang seriously underestimated enemy strength and capability. They indeed did not fully grasp the situation in Hue.

As conditions in Hue worsened, refugees fled across the Perfume River, abandoning the war-torn city.

On the scene, Gravel felt it far wiser to consolidate his already precarious position at the compound. He might otherwise risk losing his entire force in an ill-conceived effort to make contact with Truong at the Citadel. Gravel radioed General Lahue with a message to that effect. Lahue's HQ replied: "Proceed."

Gravel sent Captain Meadows's Golf Company across the Perfume River on the Nguyen Hoang Bridge that leads into Hue City proper. He left the decimated Alpha Company to defend the MACV compound. Fearing that his tanks might be too heavy to cross the bridge, Gravel left them at the LZ near the navy ramp and moved out without armor. Orders were orders, questionable or not.

Unacceptable Losses

An NVA machine gun opened up on Golf Company's lead platoon halfway across the bridge, killing or wounding ten marines. The marines funneled their fire toward the machine gun. Corporal Lester A. Tully, a Golf Company grunt [infantryman], then charged into the live fire, killed five NVAs, and silenced the machine gun. Tully's act, for which he earned the Silver Star, enabled Golf Company to make it across the river. But not much farther.

The enemy ambushed Golf Company's lead squad in the street that led to the Citadel and ARVN headquarters. From the houses to their front, the enemy blasted the marines with B-40 rockets, AK-47 automatic weapons, machine guns, and recoilless rifles. The unrelenting enemy fire pinned Golf Company in place for what seemed like forever, unable to move forward or back.

After two hours of furious fighting, Gravel's losses became unacceptable. He realized that it was impossible to continue and ordered Captain Meadows to pull back across the river. Fifty of Golf Company's 150 marines were dead or wounded. Among the casualties were Major Murphy, killed by a B-40 rocket, and Chaplain Lyons, wounded by the same rocket.

Although exhausted by the long day's fighting, a sleepless Lieutenant Colonel Gravel pondered unacceptable losses long into the night.

The Hard Way

On Thursday, February 1, 1968, the second day of fighting at Hue, Brigadier General Lahue told a UPI reporter: "Very definitely, we control the South Side of the city. I don't think that they [the NVA/VC forces] can sustain. I know they can't. I don't think they have any resupply capabilities, and once they use up what they brought in, they're finished."

The general's optimism derived more from a constant pressure from Washington to report only what leaders there wanted to hear than it did from the reality of the situation. On the plus side, however, the MACV compound and ARVN headquarters within the city remained in allied hands.

Later that morning, Gravel's marines crossed the street and secured the soccer field at Hue University, which provided the Americans—who controlled the air—with a ready-made helipad. A flow of marine reinforcements began pouring into New City at once.

While Golf and Alpha Companies held back enemy troops during February 1–3, two more marine rifle companies, three marine command groups, and another tank platoon—about one thousand men in all—arrived at the MACV compound. Captain Michael P. Downs's Fox Company, 2nd Battalion, 5th Marines, arrived on February 1, followed by Captain Ron Christmas's Hotel Company,

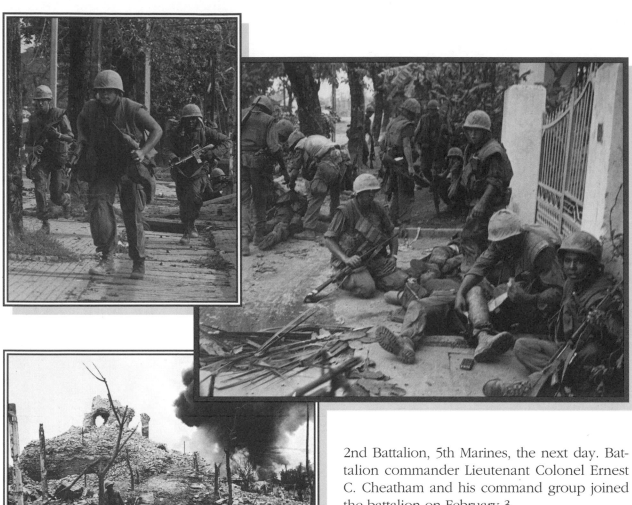

Marines dodge enemy fire (top) and tend to their wounded comrades (above, right) as fighting continues in Hue. (Above) A cloud of smoke darkens the sky above the Citadel as marines advance cautiously toward the North Vietnamese stronghold.

2nd Battalion, 5th Marines, the next day. Battalion commander Lieutenant Colonel Ernest C. Cheatham and his command group joined the battalion on February 3.

Meanwhile, for whatever reason, the Communists failed to exploit their initial advantage of superior numbers by attacking in strength at the Citadel and MACV compound. Instead, they elected to consolidate their positions on both sides of the river.

On the south bank, the Communists seized key civil buildings and military installations and sealed off residential streets with captured tanks. They converted the central hospital into a command post and turned the high school into an armory and barracks. And they further disrupted the city by releasing two thousand inmates from the municipal prison.

On the north bank, they already enjoyed the substantial benefits of a walled city designed to withstand the assaults of would-be invaders. They established their central command post within the interior walls of the well-fortified Imperial Palace. An abundance of walled gardens in residential quarters provided perfect defensive cover. And long, straight streets offered NVA defenders clear fields of fire.

The NVA/VC defenses prompted an American adviser to comment, "It would take the battleship *New Jersey* to get them out of those walls." With no battleships in sight, the marines would have to do it the hard way. No one really expected it to be easy.

Trial and Error

On the night of February 3, Lieutenant Colonel Cheatham, popularly known as Big Ernie because of his huge frame, called his company commanders together for a briefing. He wanted to start attacking the next morning at 0700 and issued crisp instructions: "Company H will seize the Public Health Building to its direct front and then support by fire the attack by Company F on the Treasury Building. Company G will be in reserve." He then reminded them that their mission was threefold:

> As you know, we have been assigned [by III MAF] to drive the NVA from the city, with minimum casualties to our own folks, and to spare as much of the city from destruction as is humanly possible. The first two tasks are easy to comprehend; the third one will be difficult to accomplish. You must dig the rats from their holes. I am authorizing you to use our direct fire weapons. Use good judgment, but protect our Marines.

Hotel Company jumped off at precisely 0700 on February 4. The 1st Platoon crossed Le Loi Street and attacked along the Perfume River, quickly seizing the building on their right front. The 3rd Platoon was then supposed to assault the Public Health Building complex, after which Company F would attack the Treasury Building under Hotel Company's covering fire. But frontal automatic-weapons fire and accurate grazing fire from the flank held up the 3rd Platoon. Captain Christmas promptly called up a 106mm recoilless rifle crew to cover 3rd Platoon's crossing. They turned the trick, as Christmas later wrote:

> I marveled at the performance of the recoilless rifle crews. They were great! These young men seemed to have no fear of the enemy fire directed at them when they rolled their weapon into the street.

> A few hours later the fighting ended for the day. Company H had successfully supported the attack on the Treasury by Company F. One more square block of Hue was returned to friendly hands.

> The Marines learned a great deal that day about fighting house to house. I quickly realized that much of the learning that day had been, and in days to come would be, through trial and error.

Maximum Force

Restraints on the use of America's vastly superior firepower severely hampered U.S. operations in Hue for almost two weeks. In an effort to limit civilian casualties and property damage, the South Vietnamese government asked the Americans to minimize their use of maximum force. Weather also became a factor, with cloudy skies and drizzling rain inhibiting U.S. air support.

These dual restrictions impeded American progress on both sides of the Perfume River, forcing the U.S. Marines to root out the enemy—house by house, street by street. The fighting dragged on, bloody and fierce, and, at times, painfully frustrating. Not until February 12—almost two weeks into the action—did the South Vietnamese government finally authorize the use of maximum force. Once unleashed, the immense U.S. arsenal of heavy weaponry proved to be both decisive and destructive.

American commanders often found it simpler and less costly to destroy buildings rather than overrun them. One marine officer said, "Some South Vietnamese are complaining about the damage to their buildings, but I have no sympathy. If you can save a marine by destroying a house to get to Charlie [NVA/VC], then I say destroy the house." Many a house fell to save a marine.

During the second half of the battle for Hue, the Americans pounded the city relentlessly with 105mm, 155mm, and 8-inch howitzer shells. Ontos vehicles mounted with 106mm recoilless rifles, self-propelled 40mm guns, and tanks cruised the streets, spearheading infantry attacks. Helicopter gunships and fighter-bombers delivered destruction from above—napalm canisters and 500- and 750-pound bombs. And from just offshore, navy destroyers and cruisers hammered the city with 5-, 6-, and 8-inch gunfire.

The enemy retaliated with automatic-weapons fire, rocketry, mortars, and fire from captured tanks. Under maximum force, Hue became a metaphor for death and destruction.

A church in the besieged city of Hue shows the extensive damage caused by U.S. firepower. Allied troops used maximum force during the fierce battle for Hue, leaving death and destruction in their wake.

Changing Colors

The next day, Big Ernie's rifle companies combined to seize the Hue Hospital from Vietcong elements. Some of the VC posed as patients. Fortunately the marines had been forewarned against possible surprises. Still, several marines took fire from Vietcong "patients." One marine narrowly averted death when a nun shot at him. The "nun" was a VC soldier dressed in a black habit. His weapon misfired. The marine's weapon did not.

In mutually supporting attacks, each company cleared an assigned section of the hospital. By the end of the day, the Hue Hospital belonged to the 2nd Battalion, 5th Marines.

That night, Lieutenant Colonel Cheatham called for another briefing. By then, the battalion had moved to within a block of the provincial capital and the city jail. A huge Vietcong flag—gold stars on red and blue—had flown from the flagpole in front of the Vietnamese Thua Thien Provincial Headquarters since January 31.

As the lieutenant colonel issued his orders for the next day, Captain Ron Christmas thought: "The sixth of February will be an eventful day for us. The old man wants us to take the capitol [sic]. It will be good to see that damn enemy flag come down."

The battle for the provincial headquarters raged for nearly five hours with the marines still unable to gain a foothold. An earlier attempt by Hotel Company to dislodge the VC using CS (tear gas) grenades failed. The marines continued to hammer away at the building with supporting arms. Captain Christmas later wrote:

A marine shuffles through debris in Hue during a search and clear mission (below) while U.S. soldiers provide cover for marines trapped under heavy fire from North Vietnamese forces (below, left).

I surveyed the situation and realized that the time had come to attack once more. The enemy's fire had slackened. I could see dead NVA soldiers in the courtyard of the building and decided to order the first platoon to attack under the cover of tear gas and smoke.

The men smashed into the building, cupping tear gas grenades in their hands. One Marine was shot and killed on the stairway, and two others were wounded, but the assault continued. They cleaned out the building, room by room, until it was theirs.

Christmas then radioed Lieutenant Colonel Cheatham and said, "We have the building, sir. We are going to run up the American flag."

The lieutenant colonel replied, "We are not authorized to fly the U.S. flag [over liberated South Vietnamese structures], but go ahead and run it up before anyone tells us not to. We are doing the fighting. We may as well have our guys get the credit. I want those NVA guys across the river to see this." Christmas did not hesitate to act on Cheatham's instructions.

Turning to Gunnery Sergeant Frank A. Thomas, Christmas said, "We have looked at the damn North Vietnamese [NLF] flag all day, and now we are going to take it down. Let's go."

Thomas "just happened" to have an American flag available for the occasion—one that until recently had flown legally over an American military compound a few blocks to the rear. Two Hotel Company riflemen had "confiscated" it along the way. At 1603, Privates First Class Walter R. Kaczmarek and Alan V. McDonald helped Gunny Thomas strike the NLF flag and hoist Old Glory in its place. Onlookers watched through wisps of tear gas, and automatic-weapons fire continued to rake the blood-splattered streets.

"When the Stars and Stripes reached the top of the pole, the gunny looked up and then burst into tears," Captain Christmas wrote. "From their positions in the building and the courtyard, the men in the company began to cheer. I was truly moved by the experience; there were tears in my eyes."

Lieutenant Colonel Cheatham radioed regimental headquarters: "Be advised we have taken the province headquarters—and somehow or other an American flag is flying over there."

Christmas knew that the U.S. flag would have to come down, but he vowed to himself that it would not be until the last U.S. Marine had left the capital grounds. Old Glory remained in place until Hotel Company moved out the next morning.

CHAPTER FIVE

The Citadel: City Without Joy

On February 2, while the marines were battling in New City and the 1st ARVN Division was holding on in the Citadel, the 3rd Brigade of the U.S. Army's 1st Air Cavalry Division air-assaulted into a landing zone six miles northwest of Hue. The 3rd Brigade was assigned the job of severing the main routes for enemy supply and infiltration. Three days later, the brigade's 2nd Battalion, 12th Cavalry, moved to seal off the city in the west and north.

After an exhausting forced march, sloshing at night through ankle-deep water, the weary 2nd Battalion soldiers seized an enemy-held hill four miles west of Hue. They immediately started shelling enemy positions in the valley below. Meanwhile, the 3rd Brigade's 5th Battalion, 7th Cavalry, swept in from the west in an attempt to link up with the 2nd Battalion. But their advance was halted by NVA units that had slipped in behind the hill held by their sister battalion.

The 2nd Battalion—which would later become known as the lost battalion—was then forced to abandon its isolated hill position and battle its way northward toward the 5th Battalion. They reached the village of Thong Bon Tri on February 9. After an all-day assault on the village, the 2nd Battalion finally succeeded in clearing the area of NVA troops.

Marines crouch in the rubble of Hue's ancient Citadel during intense combat with the North Vietnamese Army and Vietcong guerrillas.

The strong resistance encountered by the 3rd Brigade sent a message to allied commanders, however, and convinced them that reinforcements would be needed to get the job done. As a result of a conference between MACV deputy commander General Creighton W. Abrams Jr. and marine commander Lieutenant General Robert E. Cushman Jr., General Westmoreland ordered three more battalions into the area. The 1st and 2nd Battalions, 7th Cavalry, and the 101st Airborne Division's 1st Battalion, 501st Infantry—temporarily assigned to the 3rd Brigade—joined the battle for Hue.

For almost three weeks, U.S. Army forces—starting with two battalions and increasing to five—held off the NVA 24th, 29th, and 99th Regiments attempting to reinforce North Vietnamese Army and Vietcong units within the city. The U.S. Army operations outside Hue enabled the marine and ARVN troops to remain focused on operations inside Hue.

A Miracle Needed

On February 9, while American soldiers were ousting the NVA from Thong Bon Tri, the combined 1st and 5th Marines were cleaning out the remaining NVA/VC strong points in New City. By this time, Colonel Stanley S. Hughes, the regimental commander of the 1st Marines, had taken charge of all marine operations south of the Perfume River. As a product of those operations, an estimated

(Above) As fighting raged in Hue, marines battled the Communists for control of the Citadel. (Right) A young Vietcong guerrilla awaits interrogation after being captured by South Vietnamese soldiers.

1,053 enemy soldiers now lay dead in the rubbled aftermath of high-explosive warfare. But a whole lot of liberating remained to be done north of the river—block by brutal city block.

Counterattacking from their 1st Division headquarters across the river, ARVN soldiers had already recaptured the airfield and much of the northern half of the Citadel. Yet, so far, they had been unable to break through an arc of enemy strong points in the southern half. On February 10, with the struggle more than ten days old, the Communists still held 60 percent of the north bank. A broadened attack was needed to rout the strongly emplaced enemy. Again the South Vietnamese called for help. And again the marines answered their call.

This time, the 1st Battalion of the 5th Marine Regiment drew the assignment. Higher headquarters had decided to commit Major Robert H. Thompson's 1st Battalion to the battle for the Citadel on February 12, along with newly arriving ARVN marines.

This posed a problem for Thompson's marines, however, as they would be coming from Phu Bai. To reach a staging (assembly) area in New City, they would have to cross the Phu Cam Canal and move through an area not yet cleared of enemy troops. The marines held the east bank, but the NVA controlled the west. The west bank would need to be secured before 1st Battalion could cross the canal.

On the night of February 10, Lieutenant Colonel Ernie Cheatham huddled still again with Captain Ron Christmas. "Skipper, I want you to seize a bridgehead across the Phu Cam and hold it for at least twenty-four hours," Cheatham said to Hotel Company's commander. "It's the only way we can move 1/5 [1st Battalion, 5th Marines] into the action. I know your company will be outnumbered, but I'm counting on you to hold."

Christmas did not have to be told about being outnumbered. He knew about the other companies that had tried to cross the bridge only to be driven back with heavy casualties by devastating small-arms fire. "What can I do to help us across?" Christmas wondered. With all the bridges zeroed-in on by the NVA, Hotel Company would need some kind of miracle to span the canal intact.

Hotel Company Holds

Hotel Company's "miracle" was white, billowy, and hard to see through—and it went by the name of Willie Peter. Christmas, while mulling his options that evening, recalled that "the company had developed a tactic we called the 'willie-peter screen,'" as he later explained:

> We simply registered [zeroed-in] a white phosphorus (WP) round on the street about 200 meters across the bridge. After registering, we called for a concentration of WP followed by HE (high explosive fragmentation ammunition), and under

this cover crossed the bridge. The WP concealed the company's movement, while the HE made Charlie [the NVA/VC] pull in his head. Once the foothold was gained, it was expanded into an entire block.

The next day, after establishing a foothold on the west side of the canal, Captain Christmas called his platoon commanders together and said, "Hotel will hold the bridge, no matter how many enemy attack us. We've been given a job to do, and we'll do it." And they did.

Major Thompson's 1st Battalion, 5th Marines, moved through Hotel Company's bridgehead on February 12. Lieutenant Colonel Cheatham then ordered Hotel Company's marines back across the canal and placed them in reserve. But not for long.

The next day Captain Christmas led Hotel Company in an attack against an enemy base camp west of the railroad yard in New City. Christmas got caught in the open during an intense mortar barrage. He was seriously wounded and had to be evacuated. The intrepid captain later received the Navy Cross for his exemplary leadership during the Hue fighting.

Over the Edge

Major Thompson's marines entered the old city from the north on February 12, by helicopter and landing craft. They began their advance against the enemy's Citadel defenses on the left flank, with the 3rd ARVN Regiment in the center, and the South Vietnamese marines anchoring the right flank. Facing the marines were elements of the 802nd, 804th, and the K-4B NVA main force battalions—all well-trained and well-led combat troops.

Weather conditions worked against the marines at the outset, as overcast skies prevented air support during the first week of action. After two days of savage fighting, the marines remained pinned in place. Taking the Citadel was not going to be a walk in the park. Before the bitter house-to-house, alley-to-alley, street-to-street fighting for Hue ended, Thompson's battalion would lose, counting replacements, more than 100 percent of its original strength in casualties.

"Most of the battalion was either killed or wounded," British combat photographer Don McCullin recalled later. "There were only about a half dozen men in one company. I think that what happens [when death lurks around the next corner] is that one goes over the edge—you become slightly mad."

Too Much of a Bad Thing

The marines grew numb with fatigue. "On the worst days, no one expected to get through it alive," wrote journalist Michael Herr of *Esquire* magazine. His dispatches from Hue laid bare the face of battle:

A despair set in among members of the battalion that the older ones, veterans of two other wars, had never seen before. Once or twice, when the men from Graves Registration [who collected, recorded, and processed the dead] took the personal effects from the packs and pockets of dead marines, they found letters from home that had been delivered days before still unopened.

The marine wounded piled up so fast that doctors singled out the worst cases to work on but still could not keep pace with the parade of wounded. One distraught marine said, "I've seen too much of this. We've got to get some help. They're going to annihilate 1/5." They very nearly did.

End in View

By February 20, after eight straight days of fighting, Thompson's battalion had 47 marines killed, 240 badly wounded, and another 60 wounded but still fighting. But they had killed more than four times their number of dead—219 of the enemy by confirmed body count. The fighting continued. The marines edged closer to the Citadel wall, which surrounded the inner city and the moated and walled Imperial Palace.

U.S. marines drag a wounded comrade to safety. Many soldiers despaired over having to witness the deaths of so many of their fellow troops.

The next day, Lieutenant Patrick D. Polk, company commander of Alpha Company, assigned the task of securing a tower on the Citadel wall to his 2nd Platoon. Staff Sergeant James Munroe led the 2nd Platoon task force, which included a forward observer and a sniper team.

"We started about three-thirty in the morning and were told that we had two buildings to secure before we would be able to reach the tower," Munroe said later. Surprisingly, the marines met no resistance in either of the two buildings or in the tower itself. "I guess we sort of caught the NVA napping," the sergeant continued, "which was a great help."

Shortly after daybreak, the 2nd Platoon marines came under NVA sniper and rocket fire. The FO (forward observer) radioed Whiskey 1/11 (a marine artillery battalion) across the Perfume River and called in twenty rounds of variable time (VT) 4.2-inch mortar shells—airbursts. When the 11th Marine gunners ran out of VTs, they started pumping in HE and CS tear gas. The lung-searing CS drove some of the NVA troops from their holes and the marine riflemen responded.

"We did a little shooting of our own," Munroe said. "We got fifteen of them by body count from up in the tower." After that

exchange, Major Thompson ordered a renewed attack on the NVA positions along the Citadel wall.

When the assault resumed, one of the Alpha marines took a mortar hit. Lieutenant Boyd radioed to ask whether the wounded man needed evacuation. Another marine promptly replied, "Nah, we're tough down here."

Later that day, the northeast wall of the Citadel fell to Major Thompson's 1st Battalion marines. For a second time during the Hue fighting, U.S. Marines hoisted an American flag over liberated South Vietnamese soil, this time on the ramparts of the Citadel. On that same day, February 21, elements of the U.S. 1st Air Cavalry Division closed in from the west and south and cut off the last remaining enemy supply route. The end came in view.

Battle's End

Three days later, during the early hours of February 24, the Black Panther Company of the 1st ARVN Division's 2nd Battalion, 3rd Regiment, overcame the NVA defenders along the Citadel's south wall and secured the main flagpole at the Midday Gate of the Imperial Palace. At 0500, they hauled down the NLF flag and ran up the yellow-and-red standard of the Republic of Vietnam. Mop-up operations went on for several days, but the real battle was over.

(Above, right) During the Tet Offensive, marine riflemen gallantly defended their comrades against snipers. (Above) Marine gunners also played an important role in the battle, repulsing NVA forces with their deadly mortar shells.

Vietcong Death Squads

The tragedy of Hue encompassed many evils, perhaps none so despicable as the Vietcong's methodical elimination of thousands of noncombatants in the Old City. Beginning on the first day of the Communist takeover, Vietcong "death squads" roamed the streets within the walled fortress city. Seeking to use the occupation of Hue for settling old scores, they combed the city for current and past officials, civil servants, police officers, and all others known to serve or sympathize with the South Vietnamese regime. Suspected SVN agents or sympathizers were summarily executed. Most were shot, others beheaded, and still others buried alive.

The Communists went to great lengths to cover up evidence of their sinister handiwork. Douglas Pike, a U.S. Information Agency officer and recognized expert on the massacre, asserts that the killings were not random. In his 1970 study, *The Viet Cong Strategy of Terror*, Pike maintained that "virtually all were done by local Communist cadres," as distinguished from NVA soldiers. Information revealed in later years indicates that the Vietcong targeted their victims from lists of so-called enemies of the people compiled beforehand by intelligence agents.

Most of the slayings, as Pike further noted, were carried out in secrecy "with extraordinary effort made to hide the bodies." For that reason, the exact number of slaughtered civilians will likely never be known. Pike estimated that as many as fifty-seven hundred people may have been slain in Hue while the Communists occupied the city.

At battle's end, official records showed 5,113 NVA/VC dead in Hue, with another 89 captured. No accounting was made for the number of enemy wounded or those who died of injuries. The ARVN casualties totaled 384 killed and 1,830 wounded. Some 5,800 civilians were listed as dead or missing, most of whom had been killed by Communist death squads and buried in mass graves in the inner city. The U.S. Army losses numbered 74 dead and 507 seriously wounded. Finally, the Marine Corps reported 147 men killed and 857 seriously wounded—about half of the marine infantrymen committed to the battle in Hue.

Officially, the ARVN 1st Division received credit for taking the Citadel. Major Thompson had witnessed the Black Panthers in action and held them in high regard. His esteem for the Panthers, however, did not carry over to the rest of the ARVN soldiers. For that reason, Thompson felt pleased that the Black Panthers had been selected over lesser ARVN units to raise their country's flag at the Citadel.

As far as where credit for taking the Citadel *really* belonged, Major Thompson held to his own thoughts on the matter: "The MACV records will reflect that the ARVN, assisted by 1/5, took

While holding a baby, a young girl stands in the shambles of her home following the devastating Vietcong attack.

the Citadel. That was strictly public relations hogwash, like so much that MACV put out during the war. The 1st Battalion, 5th Marines took the Citadel. The ARVN were spectators."

To the peace-loving people of Hue—victimized by a war not of their making—it mattered little whether ARVN soldiers or U.S. Marines received the credit for "liberating" their city. When the flames of war turned into ashes and the last crackle of automatic-weapons fire echoed off into history, the ancient city of Hue lay in shambles—a city without joy.

CHAPTER SIX

Khe Sanh Revisited: The Real Pain

"**W**e huddled together in the bunker, shoulders high and necks pulled in to leave no space between helmet and flak jacket," wrote *Newsweek* reporter John Donnelly. "There is no describing an artillery barrage. The earth shakes, clods of dirt fall from the ceiling, and shrapnel makes a repulsive singing through the air."

Donnelly might have also noted that in terms of sheer terror nothing exceeds the frightful effect of artillery's big bang on the human psyche. The horror transmitted by the enormity of pure noise alone defies the power of human imagination to define. In the company of such dreadful fright, of skittering rats and unwashed bodies, of smoldering heaps of garbage and human waste, dwelled the marines of Khe Sanh for seventy-seven days.

Hill 861A

Shortly after 0400 on February 5, 1968, the grunts of Echo Company, 2nd Battalion, 26th Marines, heard the baritone *thonking* of NVA mortar shells leaving their tubes. Seconds later, 82mm missiles exploded across Echo's sandbagged bunkers, trenches, and foxholes on Hill 861A. Steel fragments whizzed through the air. And showers of fine red clay rained down upon the bearded, unwashed marines assigned to cover the Rao Quan River valley approach to the Khe Sanh Combat Base. A barrage of RPGs (rocket-propelled grenades) followed, fired off by hordes of NVAs moving in to the attack. The mortar rounds and RPGs wiped out many of the crew-served weapons on Hill 861 Alpha.

Marines from Echo Company search for enemy forces on one of the hills near Khe Sanh Combat Base. When the NVA/VC forces reinitiated their attack on Khe Sanh, Echo Company took a beating from the Communists before regaining control of the hill.

A number of marines were killed or wounded, primarily because Echo Company had not occupied the hill long enough to become well entrenched. NVA sappers with explosive charges blew huge holes in the barbed-wire barriers that rimmed the hill. Captain Earle G. Breeding's Echo Company marines clutched their weapons and waited for the enemy to make contact.

Across the valley to the southeast of Hill 861A, two hundred artillery shells hammered into the KSCB. Colonel David E. Lownds called all units to Red Alert—100 percent readiness. Lownds felt sure that the long-promised threat of an all-out NVA attack was about to become a reality. He was mistaken. The huge barrage directed against the combat base served only to divert attention from the battalion-size attack on 861A.

The NVA troops, who seemed to know beforehand the layout of Echo's defensive positions, struck first at Lieutenant Edmund R. Shanley's 1st Platoon. Wearing bush hats and tennis shoes, a swarm of North Vietnamese— running full tilt and firing AK-47s—breached the perimeter wire and plunged into Echo's trench line. In an age of modern weaponry and electronic warfare, the ensuing clash of warriors reverted to a purely primitive struggle for survival. A wild melee of swinging fists, knives, rifle butts, and bayonets ruled the mist- and fog-shrouded morning.

Corporal Billy E. Drexel, a mortar section leader, exposed himself to heavy fire moving one of his squads into a fire-support position. Private First Class Newton D. Lyle, a member of the mortar squad, recalled:

> We went over there and you could actually see the [NVAs] running around on the lines, laughing [many were high on marijuana or opium] and throwing [grenades] in bunkers, and you could hear the screams of your buddies, your friends, and we was running around out there firing mortar rounds out in front of the wires, and after a while they come and told us that all the men had been wiped out in the trenches directly in front of us and we was to fire directly into the trenches.

With Echo Company's situation growing momentarily more in doubt, the regimental fire-support coordination center called on the big guns for help—105s and 155s. A B-52 strike followed. Lima Company commander Dick Camp, who watched the attack unfold from the main compound, recalled:

The massive pinpoint artillery and air response sealed the NVA breakthrough from the rear—prevented a follow-on battalion from scaling the hill—while Echo Company fought back against the badly hurt NVA battalion that had penetrated its position. This is not to say that the bitter fighting was not touch and go, for we almost lost Echo Company, but the survivors held until dawn, threw the NVA off the hill, and even weathered a follow-on attack the NVA launched through the thick morning fog.

In their final struggle to kick the enemy off the hill and regain lost positions, the Echo Company grunts proved to be better street fighters than the NVA intruders. After the battle for Hill 861A, Captain Breeding proudly described the action:

> The M-16 [U.S. 5.56 mm rifle] didn't come into play too much because of the hill we were on. There were really no fields of fire to speak of, and it turned out to be a hand grenade war. And then when Charlie [NVA] got inside the wire it was just like a World War II movie with . . . knife-fighting, bayonet fighting, hitting people on the nose with your fist and all the rest of that, and Charlie didn't know how to cope with it all. We just walked all over him once we were able to close with him [close enough for hand-to-hand combat].

The official marine account of the action lists 109 enemy as KIA (killed in action). Other counts showed as many as 150 NVA dead. Seven Echo Company marines were killed and another 35

Marines rush to board a helicopter as artillery shells pound Khe Sanh Combat Base.

seriously wounded. Captain Breeding maintained that none of his dead marines had been killed in the hand-to-hand fighting but rather as a result of the enemy bombardment. Charlie had taken a drubbing on Hill 861A. Two nights later, he would fare better at Lang Vei.

The Sound of Treads

The Special Forces (Green Berets) camp at Lang Vei stood isolated in heavily wooded, craggy terrain, eight kilometers southwest of the Khe Sanh Combat Base. It was staffed by twenty-four Green Berets and four hundred montagnards (hill people). Lang Vei formed a base of operations for reconnaissance missions along the Ho Chi Minh Trail and guerrilla operations across the border in Laos. All hope of holding the camp against the much larger NVA forces resided with American artillery support in Khe Sanh and marine fighter-bombers in Da Nang. They would not be sufficient to stem the surging forces of the NVA.

At 0030 on February 7, a sudden flash of light from an activated trip flare alerted Sergeant Nikolas Fragos, an assistant medical specialist at Lang Vei, to movement in the barbed-wire perimeter. Nearly blinded by the flare, Fragos squinted into the dazzling light from his post atop an observation tower above the tactical operations center (TOC). He saw two NVA soldiers with wire cutters, calmly snipping a path through the protective wire. A burst of defensive friendly fire chopped down both of them in an instant. Behind their fallen bodies, Fragos could make out the forbidding hulks of two olive-green mechanized monsters—*tanks*!

Fragos immediately radioed the command bunker: "We have tanks in our wire!" It was the first time ever in the Vietnam War that the Communists had deployed armor against the Americans.

Camp commander Captain Frank C. Willoughby, USA, could not believe it. Rumors had had it that the NVA might be moving armored vehicles into the area, but no one suspected the enemy of having tanks. Willoughby ran up the steps of his CP bunker to see for himself. Sure enough, two Soviet-made PT-76 light tanks were clanking and crunching their way forward, blasting away with their 76 mm guns, crushing bunkers and everything else in their paths.

Two enemy platoons armed with AK-47s and flamethrowers moved forward behind the tanks. Then a third tank appeared, followed by two more. The defenders knocked out the first three tanks, but the other two crashed and smashed about inside the perimeter wire, dishing out destruction. Two more PT-76s rumbled into the camp from the north. Four more tanks penetrated the wire in the west. Willoughby called desperately for help.

Fifteen minutes later, artillery from Khe Sanh began hammering the attackers. Fighter-bombers arrived from Da Nang ten minutes later and struck again and again from above. Willoughby called Khe Sanh for help from marine ground troops. But with KSCB itself under heavy artillery and mortar fire, Colonel Lownds, fearing a ground assault on the main base at any moment, denied Willoughby's request. Lownds's decision was later upheld as having been correct under the circumstances. Unhappily for Willoughby and his troops, they had been left to shift for themselves.

The Lang Vei defenders fought valiantly for more than twenty-four hours before being overrun on the morning of February 8. Fourteen Special Forces troops either had been evacuated by helicopter in the daylight or had escaped to Khe Sanh during the second night. Ten were killed. Of the approximately four hundred montagnards, two hundred had been killed or wounded. Seventy-five more were listed as missing. The camp itself had been reduced to smoking ruins.

The marines disclaimed any direct connection between the assault on Lang Vei and the siege of Khe Sanh. But the presence of enemy tanks at the Special Forces camp sent a shiver down the collective spine of the Khe Sanh marines. As *Esquire* journalist Michael Herr pointed out, "After Lang Vei how could you look out of your perimeter at night without hearing the treads coming?"

Soldiers begin rebuilding the village of Lang Vei after it was nearly destroyed by allied and NVA/VC fighting.

"Smashing the Enemy Snake"

On the night of February 8, 1968, a Radio Hanoi broadcaster reviewed an article that had appeared that day in *Quan Doi Nhan Dan*, the official paper of the North Vietnamese People's Army. The reviewer stressed that Lang Vei had been "a first-rate annihilation battle," providing a "very good example of how well . . . regular units can conduct a lightning, neat attack, and how quickly they can take control of the battlefield."

Earlier that same day, Radio Hanoi had broadcast a summary of a similar but longer news piece from the People's Army paper:

The Lang Vei victory is a striking example by the main force Liberation Armed Forces of quick attack, complete annihilation, and holding the initiative on the battlefield. With a determination to fight and close coordination from various armed branches, the Liberation Armed Forces, coming from many directions and various points, quickly divided the enemy, destroyed position after position, and in a short time annihilated a strong U.S. defensive position. That was a strong blow smashing the enemy snake, cutting defensive Route 9, and throwing the enemy into great turmoil.

Waiting for the Big One

The fall of Lang Vei cleared a path for an NVA move against the Khe Sanh Combat Base itself. During the early morning darkness of February 9, strong elements of the NVA 325C Division attacked Hill 64, a small knob southwest of the KSCB airstrip held by the 1st Battalion, 9th Marines. Was this finally the "big" attack? No. Although the marines surrendered the hill in the dark, they launched a vicious counterattack in the daylight and regained the hill. Twenty-one marines were killed in what turned out to be only a brief encounter. The North Vietnamese left 134 of their own dead on Hill 64.

The next ground attack came on February 21. A battalion-size NVA force assaulted the 37th ARVN Ranger Battalion positions on the east end of the compound. The South Vietnamese soldiers repelled the attack handily. The rangers fought admirably, took few casualties, and killed twenty to twenty-five enemy troops. Again, the big one remained only an anticipation.

On February 23, Lieutenant Donald J. Jacques led a patrol from his 3rd Platoon of Bravo Company, 1st Battalion, 26th Marines, to locate and eliminate an NVA mortar that was shelling the base with deadly accuracy. The patrol came under fire in open ground. Outflanked and outgunned by the enemy, Jacques ordered his men to return to base, about 200 meters (219 yards) away. Of the original twenty-nine patrol members, four made it back. Lieutenant Jacques was not among them. Four weeks under constant shelling would pass before Bravo Marines could recover their twenty-five buddies, lying dead beyond the perimeter.

Another serious NVA effort to breach the KSCB perimeter came on February 29. Amid rumors that the Communists were tunneling up to and under the KSCB compound for a final assault, the NVA struck the ARVN ranger positions again. The rangers fended off the enemy with automatic-weapons fire, exploding Claymore mines, and flesh-shredding grenades. After three unsuccessful thrusts at the rangers, the NVA soldiers withdrew, leaving seventy of their dead strung out in the perimeter wire. Still no big one.

Lima Company skipper Dick Camp recalled that he and others at KSCB "started kidding that one day we were going to wake up and find that the North Vietnamese had erected their own barbed-wire fence and watchtowers and that we would be ensconced in the Khe Sanh prison camp." Camp also recalled that the marines kept a sense of humor while they awaited the big attack:

We had a little sign over the Alpha COC [combat operations center] that was blank on one side and said on the other, "Tonight's the night." On those nights [that] we expected to get an infantry assault against our position, we turned the sign over so it could be read. After a while, it remained undisturbed, with the message side out.

Casualties mounted from the incessant shelling, but the big one—the all-out North Vietnamese ground assault on the Khe Sanh Combat Base—never came.

A Fitting End

In the wake of the Tet Offensive, General Westmoreland ordered the U.S. 1st Air Cavalry Division to relieve the marines at Khe Sanh. Operation Pegasus—code name for the relief operation (after the fabled winged horse of Greek mythology)—commenced on April 1. Reinforced by units of the 1st Marine Division and the South Vietnamese Airborne Brigade, the 2nd Battalion, 7th Cavalry, linked up with marine and ARVN elements pushing out from Khe Sanh at 1350 on April 6. Two days later, at 0800 on April 8, the 3rd Brigade of the 1st Air Cavalry Division officially relieved the marines.

The marines rejected the notion that they had needed to be relieved from a place that they had not wanted to defend in the first place. They felt that Westmoreland had sent the 1st Air Cavalry to relieve them only to make the army look good. As proof of their continued viability as a fighting organization, the 3rd Battalion, 26th Marines, seized Hill 881 North on Easter Sunday, six days after their "relief."

In the aftermath of that final encounter with the marines, the enemy began pulling its forces out of the area. The marines' seizure of 881N marked a fitting end to the "siege" of Khe Sanh.

The Horror of War

In seventy-seven days at Khe Sanh, 205 U.S. Marines were killed and more than 1,500 were wounded.

(Below) Although NVA/VC troops continued to besiege Khe Sanh Combat Base, they failed to launch a massive ground assault. (Below, left) Troops en route to Khe Sanh probe for mines during Operation Pegasus.

Beating Down the Enemy

To call the defense of Khe Sanh a "siege" is something of a misnomer, as it implies a blockade. At no time during the stand-off at Khe Sanh was the enemy able to prevent the daily flow of supplies into the compound. The principal carrier used in the airlift was the C-130 Hercules, ably assisted by C-123 Providers, C-7A Caribous, and CH-46 Sea Knight helicopters. From January 21 through April 8, food, ammunition, and supplies airlifted into the KSCB totaled 12,400 tons—hardly indicative of an effective blockade.

Nor was it only the marines who were under "siege" at Khe Sanh in the sense of being under persistent attack. American tactical aircraft—A-4 Skyhawks, A-6A Intruders, F-4 Phantoms, and F-105 Thunderchiefs—flew more than three hundred sorties daily, delivering a total of thirty-five thousand tons of bombs on suspected enemy targets. Flying about forty-five daily sorties from bases in Guam, Thailand, and Okinawa, B-52 Stratofortresses further devastated the enemy with bomb loads totaling 110,000 tons.

The B-52s could be neither seen nor heard from the ground. Their presence over an area first became known by the whistling sound of their descending bombs. The Communists called them "the Whispering Death." One Khe Sanh bunker dweller recalled, "All you saw was the air being ripped apart and the ground tremoring underneath you—and you bouncing in the air."

Beyond this devastating display of aerial force, American artillery pummeled the enemy around the clock every day. If the engagement at Khe Sanh can accurately be termed a siege, it seems fair to ask just who laid siege to whom?

As III MAF commander Lieutenant General Cushman observed, "The trouble is that everybody counts the *incoming* rounds. No one ever counts the *outgoing*. We replied a hundred-fold to every enemy shell. We beat them down. The area was becoming untenable for the enemy."

During the Tet Offensive, F-105 Thunderchiefs (pictured) and other tactical aircraft pummeled enemy targets with a total of thirty-five thousand tons of bombs.

While reliable enemy casualty figures are unavailable, the NVA left 1,602 dead bodies on the battlefield. General Westmoreland estimated that the enemy lost between 10,000 and 15,000 troops during that eleven-week standoff.

The long ordeal at Khe Sanh had cut across the spectrum of humankind's ability to wage war. Slightly more than six thousand defenders had fought off approximately twenty thousand attackers for seventy-seven days and had in the end prevailed. The conflict demonstrated the efficiency of electronic weaponry, massive airlifts of matériel, tactical air support—Khe Sanh had become the most bombed target in military history—and the troublesome truth that hand-to-hand fighting still forms a crude but necessary part of war, even in this modern age. More than anything, perhaps, it pierced the hearts and seared the souls of all who took part, and left all with a personal void of sorts.

In the words of Ray W. Stubbe, who saw it all at Khe Sanh as the Lutheran chaplain of the 1st Battalion, 26th Marines:

> Each and every man left a part of himself at Khe Sanh. Khe Sanh in turn left a part of itself inside of us.

> I hurt then and I still hurt today, but it is from the pain that I have gained an awareness of war's real change. The real pain is not on the battlefield, it is on the land and the people afterwards. Nothing can extinguish the horror of war.

Wounded marines huddle beneath their ponchos while awaiting medical assistance. Fifteen hundred marines were wounded in the fighting at Khe Sanh, and another 205 lost their lives.

AFTERWORD

The Meaning of Tet

The siege of Khe Sanh started before and continued long after the Tet Offensive. But like Tet, it was inextricably tied to North Vietnam's grand battle plan known to the Communists as *Tong Cong Kich, Tong Khai Nghia*—"General Offensive, General Uprising." Shortened by the Communists to TCK-TKN, this plan, when implemented, became known to the world as the Tet Offensive. Tet, however, represented only the second phase of a three-phase military operation devised by General Vo Nguyen Giap.

Giap's Lever

The first phase of Giap's "lever," as the Communists called Giap's concept, commenced prior to Tet. Brigadier General Davidson, General Westmoreland's intelligence chief, outlined Giap's lever this way:

> In Phase I of the plan (late fall 1967), United States forces were to be drawn into the peripheries of South Vietnam by a series of attacks along the borders of the country. Giap's Phase II (the Tet offensive) foresaw the attacks on the cities which would bring about the disintegration of ARVN and the rallying of the South Vietnamese people to the Viet Cong banners. This sudden shift in allegiance would overthrow the Thieu government and isolate the American forces in their bases. By this time, according to Giap's plan, the United States troops would be confused, hemmed in, and demoralized, thereby setting the stage for Giap's final blow. Then would come Phase III. Giap would overwhelm Khe Sanh with two, three, or four NVA divisions, ending the war with a stunning military victory.

General Vo Nguyen Giap (far left) visits one of his antiaircraft units during the Tet Offensive. After the NVA defeat at Khe Sanh, Giap's offensive plan was abandoned.

In this broader sense, Khe Sanh formed an inseparable part of the Tet Offensive, which most historical sources confine to the period from January 30 through February 24, 1968. Khe Sanh was to have become the arena for that decisive set-piece battle that both sides had contemplated for so long. But events took a different turn during and after Phase II of Giap's lever.

Winning and Losing

The armed forces of the United States and South Vietnam, as well as other friendly forces, fought magnificently during the Tet Offensive. In every village, town, and city, and on every front from the DMZ to the Mekong Delta, the allied forces won stunning military victories under appalling conditions. Aside from about a dozen major targets—including Saigon, Hue, and Khe Sanh—the Communists were turned away from their objectives within a week.

The second phase of TCK-TKN—the Tet Offensive—had failed. Giap, in waiting until the last minute to issue attack orders, had stripped his units of coordination. Confusion over the starting date had further robbed them of surprise. In spreading his forces so thinly, across such broad expanse, Giap had violated the cardinal principle of military strategy—concentration of force. Moreover, he had been wrong in thinking that the South Vietnamese army would collapse and that the people would rise in revolt. Lastly, General Westmoreland's eleventh-hour decision to move troops closer to the cities reinforced the urban centers and also severed Communist reinforcement routes.

Similar but Different

"**M**ore drivel has been written and televised about Khe Sanh than about any other episode of Indochina War II [the Vietnam War]." So wrote Brigadier General Phillip B. Davidson, the U.S. intelligence chief in Vietnam during the Tet Offensive.

The press and television made countless comparisons between Khe Sanh and the French stronghold at Dien Bien Phu. In February 1968, Walter Cronkite, the esteemed anchor of the evening news on CBS, told a radio audience: "The parallels are there for all to see." And there *were* some obvious similarities.

"The NVA surrounded both garrisons with superior numbers," Brigadier General Davidson explained. "The enemy held the ground around the bases from which he could pour artillery and mortar fire on the French and American positions, and both garrisons depended entirely on air for resupply." What usually went unnoticed—or at least unreported—by the news media were the differences between the two situations. Davidson continued:

> The two factors which had finally proved fatal to the French at Dien Bien Phu, were Giap's superior artillery and mortar firepower and his ability to cut the aerial supply line into the garrison. Giap never had the firepower advantage at Khe Sanh, nor anything close to it. The Americans' combined air power and external artillery fire gave Westmoreland a tremendous predominance in destructive capacity. While Giap theoretically had the capacity to sever, or at least severely inhibit, air resupply to Khe Sanh, he never did so.

In sum, the differences between Khe Sanh and Dien Bien Phu exceeded their similarities and made for opposite outcomes on the battlefield.

During the Battle of Dien Bien Phu, the Vietnamese crippled the French by cutting their aerial supply lines. However, during the assault on Khe Sanh, supply planes continued to drop rations and war supplies into the beleaguered base (pictured).

Although the combined allied forces suffered losses of 2,600 killed and 12,727 wounded, their casualty figures were dwarfed by those of the enemy. Of some 84,000 Communist troops committed to the fighting, more than 45,000 were killed. (Some estimates place the number of Communist dead higher than 60,000.) The Vietcong took most of the losses and thereafter virtually ceased to exist.

Government figures showed 7,721 civilian deaths, with 18,516 wounded. Tet created another 670,000 refugees and caused an estimated $173 million in property losses. Militarily, however, the Communists suffered a monumental defeat.

In the end, the United States and South Vietnam had won the battles, but they had lost the war.

A South Vietnamese soldier urges villagers to continue past the bullet-riddled bodies of Vietcong guerrillas. An estimated forty-five thousand Communists were killed during the Tet Offensive, with the Vietcong taking the brunt of the losses.

The High Point

Back in the United States, the reality of a great allied victory and a disastrous Communist defeat was never conveyed by the American media to the people dependent upon it to report the true situation in Vietnam. The American will to persist in a seemingly unwinnable war faltered. How could the American public believe government reports that U.S. forces were winning in Vietnam while the media portrayed Tet as a great Hanoi victory? Perhaps General William Childs Westmoreland himself best stated the case for truth in reporting when he wrote:

> Despite the fact that the North Vietnamese and Viet Cong incurred a military defeat of such proportions that it took them four years to recover, reporting of the [Tet] offensive by the press and television in the United States gave an impression if not of American and South Vietnamese defeat, then of an endless war that could never be won. Even a number of senior officials in Washington were deceived, failing to heed the fact that historically an enemy who is losing may launch a desperate effort to reverse the tide of battle, as in the German offensives of 1918 and in the Battle of the Bulge [in 1944–1945]. Halting the bombing of most of North Vietnam, President Johnson removed himself from the political arena, which led to political negotiations in Paris; but the negotiations were for long years meaningless, achieving little more than to decide the shape of the conference table. Yet the war went on, and more American soldiers were killed while their enemy ostensibly parlayed peace in Paris that had been killed before the negotiations in Paris began.

U.S. soldiers land in the Mekong Delta. When the Vietnam War ended in April 1975, 47,244 Americans had been killed.

Phase III of TCK-TKN—the great set-piece battle at Khe Sanh—collapsed under the weight of Communist losses during the Tet Offensive and never took place. The North Vietnamese withdrew their forces from the Khe Sanh area in April 1968; the Americans evacuated and abandoned the Khe Sanh Combat Base two months later. General Westmoreland rotated home in June 1968.

The killing fields of Vietnam continued to yield a harvest of death and human misery for another seven years. On April 30, 1975, the NVA entered Saigon, finally ending a war that claimed 47,244 American lives in battle, and an overall total of 1,078,162 American casualties.

Within the larger context of that horrid ten-year war, the Tet Offensive stands out as the high point of American achievement in Vietnam. American hopes for ultimately winning the Vietnam War went downhill from there. Such was the meaning of Tet.

Appendix: Portfolio of Aircraft, Arms, and Armor

AK-47 rifle: The Soviet-pattern 7.62mm assault rifle, with the Chinese copy, the T-56, became the standard infantry weapon of the North Vietnamese Army and the Vietcong. The AK-47 fires either single shot or on full automatic. Simple to operate and easy to maintain, it was a most effective weapon in Vietnam.

artillery: Known as the "king of battle," artillery played an important part in maintaining U.S. firepower supremacy over the enemy in Vietnam. Artillery weaponry used by the Americans in Vietnam consisted mainly of 105mm and 155mm towed artillery, self-propelled 105mm and 155mm howitzers, 175mm guns, 8-inch howitzers, and aerial rockets. Naval gunfire support comprised 5-, 6-, and 8-inch guns. Communist artillery mainstays included 76mm, 85mm, 100mm, 122mm, 130mm, and 152mm guns and howitzers, and 140mm rockets.

B-40 rocket: Soviet-pattern rocket-propelled grenade; standard shoulder-fired Communist rocket (*see also* rocket-propelled grenade).

B-52 Stratofortress: The Boeing B-52 Stratofortress is an eight-jet, swept-wing, long-range heavy bomber, developed for the U.S. Air Force and first flown in 1952. It carries a crew of six and a bomb load of sixty thousand pounds in various ordnance combinations. The B-52 flies at a speed of over 650 mph to a range of 12,500 miles. It is armed with four .50-caliber machine guns in a rear turret.

C 4: A plastic explosive compound.

C-7A Caribou: The Canadian De Havilland DHC-4 Caribou—designated C-7A by the U.S. Air Force—is a twin-engine (piston) light tactical transport in service with about a dozen countries. First flown in 1958, it carries a crew of two hundred and thirty-two troops. The Caribou flies at a top speed of 182 mph.

C-123 Provider: The Fairchild C-123 Provider is a twin-engine assault transport developed for the U.S. Air Force and first flown in 1954. The C-123K version is fitted with two jet engines to provide short-takeoff-and-landing (STOL) capability. It has a range of 1,035 miles and can reach a speed of 173 mph with sixty-one troops aboard.

C-130 Hercules: The Lockheed C-130 Hercules is a four-engine (turboprop) medium assault transport developed for the U.S. Air Force and first flown in 1954. It carries ninety-two fully equipped troops at a maximum speed of 368 mph. The Hercules, with a range of 4,700 miles, was the "workhorse" aircraft used during the siege of Khe Sanh.

CH-46 Sea Knight: The Boeing Vertol CH-46 or UH-46 Sea Knight is a transport and utility helicopter used by the U.S. Navy and Marine Corps. First flown in 1958, it carries twenty-five troops and flies at a speed of 161 mph.

Claymore mine: The M18A1 Antipersonnel (Claymore) mine comprises a rectangular cast-iron box with spikes fitted to its base for stability. Placed with its face toward the enemy, it explodes unidirectionally, releasing some seven hundred steel balls in a sixty-degree fan-shaped pattern to a lethal distance of fifty yards. The mine can be detonated either by tripwire or by remote control.

CS: Nonlethal tear gas.

Duster: An armored tracked vehicle of World War II vintage, usually fitted with twin 40mm cannons.

fléchette: A small dart-shaped projectile; clustered in artillery shells and bombs, or shot from guns.

grenade: A small explosive or chemical missile of varied design. Grenades may be classified as hand or rifle grenades. More recently grenades have been designed to be projected from special grenade launchers (*see also* rocket-propelled grenade).

HE: High-explosive fragmentation ordnance.

helicopter gunship: An assault helicopter equipped with a variety of add-on armaments, including rockets and machine guns. One of the more formidable helicopter gunships was the Bell AH-1 Cobra, introduced in Vietnam in 1967. Of narrow silhouette, the Cobra carried a bow-mounted 40mm grenade launcher and minigun (a multibarreled rapid-firing machine gun) and wing pods of machine guns and rockets.

M-16 rifle: The U.S. 5.56mm M16A1 rifle replaced the 7.62mm M-14 rifle in 1967 as the standard infantry weapon in Vietnam. It is an air-cooled, gas-operated, magazine-fed automatic or semiautomatic rifle with an effective range of 460 meters (503 yards). The M-16 weighs 7.4 pounds and is 39 inches long. It can fire 650 to 850 rounds per minute.

M-48 tank: This U.S. medium tank of the Patton series weighs fifty-two tons, has a maximum speed of 30 mph, and armament consisting of a 90mm gun (with a range of about 12 miles), and a turret-mounted .50-caliber machine gun with a coaxial .30-caliber machine gun.

M-60 machine gun: The U.S. M-60 7.62mm general purpose machine gun (GPMG) is gas operated, bipod- or tripod-mounted, belt fed, and fully automatic. This standard American machine gun has a cyclic rate of fire of 550 rounds per minute and a maximum effective range of 875 yards with a bipod and 940 yards with a tripod. The M-60 operates best within 109 yards.

M-72: The U.S. M-72 is a light assault weapon (LAW); standard shoulder-fired 66mm antitank rocket; an unguided missile with a range of five hundred to six hundred yards.

medevac: To evacuate casualties; a medical evacuation helicopter.

mortars: Mortars are high-angle fire weapons, particularly suited for use in the hilly terrain surrounding Khe Sanh. U.S. forces used 60mm (light), 81mm (medium), and 4.2-inch (heavy) mortars. The North Vietnamese Army and Vietcong forces used 61mm, 82mm, and 120mm mortars. In that the 61mm and the 82mm mortar bores were slightly larger than their U.S. equivalents, the NVA and VC could fire captured U.S. ammunition.

106mm recoilless rifle: The M-40A1 106mm recoilless rifle is a large-caliber, lightweight, flexible infantry weapon. It is especially effective in providing added punch in house-to-house fighting (as in Hue). Recoil is eliminated by the controlled release of propellant gases to the rear through a breech-block opening. The M-40 is usually mounted (rather than lugged about) on jeeps or other vehicles, such as the Ontos.

Ontos: The U.S. Marine Corps M-50 Ontos is a full-track, self-propelled, direct-fire, and antitank weapons system. It is armed with six 106mm recoilless rifles, one .30-caliber machine gun, and four .50-caliber spotting rifles. The Ontos carries a crew of three at a speed of 30 mph over a range of 150 miles.

PT-76 tank: A Soviet-supplied light amphibious tank, the PT-76 appeared for the first time in Vietnam during the Tet Offensive, when it was used to overrun the Special Forces camp at Lang Vei. The PT-76 weighs 13.78 tons, mounts a 76mm cannon and a 7.62mm machine gun, while protecting a crew of three with armor plating of 11 to 14mm. It has a top speed of 27 mph and a range of 155 miles on land; on water, 6.25 mph and 62.5 miles, respectively.

rocket-propelled grenade (RPG): A grenade launched from a portable rocket launcher and propelled by a small rocket motor (*see also* B-40 rocket).

trip flare: An illumination flare set off by a tripwire.

VT: A variable-time fuze designed to detonate artillery shells, bombs, mines, or other charges by external influence other than contact in the target area.

WP: "Willie Peter"; white phosphorus, a chemical used in grenades and artillery shells, primarily to provide a smoke screen.

Glossary

ARVN: Army of the Republic of (South) Vietnam.

attrition: a gradual reduction of personnel.

battalion: a body of troops made up of headquarters and two or more companies or batteries.

battery: a grouping of artillery pieces for tactical purposes.

brigade: a military unit smaller than a division and larger than a regiment, with attached groups and/or battalions as needed to meet anticipated requirements.

Bronze Star: U.S. award for bravery in combat (when worn with a "V" on the ribbon) ranking below a Silver Star.

bunker: a fortified structure for the protection of personnel and armament (such as machine guns) in a defensive position.

Camp J. J. Carroll: a U.S. firebase east of Khe Sanh.

Capital Military Region: the seat of the South Vietnamese government and the headquarters of MACV and many other U.S. units, located in Saigon and Gia Dinh Province within III Corps.

Central Executive Committee: the sixty-four-member governing body of the National Liberation Front.

Charlie: popular nickname for a Vietcong guerrilla soldier.

Citadel: the moat- and wall-enclosed Old City or Imperial City section of Hue (*see also* New City).

Combined Action Company: a joint American Marine/South Vietnamese militia unit established to protect a specific village.

CP: command post.

CTZ: combat tactical zone.

Democratic Republic of Vietnam: North Vietnam; now (since July 2, 1976) known as the Socialist Republic of Vietnam.

Dien Bien Phu: site in North Vietnam of the climactic battle that ended the war between France and North Vietnam in 1954.

division: a tactical combat unit or formation larger than a regiment or brigade but smaller than a corps.

DMZ: demilitarized zone established by the Geneva accords in 1954. Six miles wide, the zone roughly divided North and South Vietnam along the 17th parallel. The accords specified that no military activities were to take place within the zone.

firefight: a brief intense exchange of fire between infantry units.

flak jacket: a jacket of heavy fabric containing metal plates for protection against flak (shrapnel).

FO: forward observer; one who directs air strikes, artillery and mortar fire, and the like, from a front-line position.

foxhole: a small hole used for cover and to fight out of by one or two people.

General Offensive, General Uprising: *see* TCK-TKN.

Giap's lever: Communist name for the three-pronged attack devised by General Vo Nguyen Giap to implement TCK-TKN.

Green Berets: *see* Special Forces.

grunt: popular nickname for a marine combat infantryman.

guerrilla: one who engages in irregular warfare, usually acting independently and in small groups.

Hanoi: capital of the Socialist Republic of Vietnam (formerly North Vietnam).

helipad: helicopter landing pad.

Ho Chi Minh Trail: the vital Vietcong supply line that started in North Vietnam, passed through Laos and Cambodia, and forked off into various destinations in South Vietnam.

Hue: the capital of Thua Thien Province and former imperial capital of Vietnam.

Joint Chiefs of Staff: a U.S. military advisory group comprising the chiefs of staff of the army and air force, the chief of naval operations, and the commandant of the marine corps.

kamikaze: a Japanese pilot or explosive-laden plane assigned to a suicidal crash dive into an enemy target (such as a ship) during World War II.

Khe Sanh: site of a marine corps combat base located fifteen miles south of the DMZ near the Laotian border; also a village adjacent to the combat base.

KIA: killed in action.

kilometer: five-eighths (.62) of a mile.

KSCB: Khe Sanh Combat Base.

Lang Vei: Special Forces camp near Khe Sanh.

listening post: a small sentry post outlying a main fortification.

LOC: line of communication.

LZ: landing zone.

MAAG: the U.S. Military Assistance Advisory Group, formed on November 1, 1955, to provide assistance to the Republic of Vietnam.

MACV: Military Assistance Command, Vietnam; the U.S. command over all U.S. activities in Vietnam, originated in 1962.

Medal of Honor: highest U.S. award for bravery in combat.

montagnards: Vietnamese hill people organized by U.S. Special Forces to engage in guerrilla activities against the NVA and VC.

MP: military police.

National Liberation Front: the NLF; officially the National Front for the Liberation of the South. Formed on December 20, 1960, the NLF aimed to overthrow South Vietnam's government and reunite the south with the north. Its members included both Communists and non-Communists.

Navy Cross: second-highest U.S. Navy and Marine Corps award for bravery in combat.

New City: the more Westernized, basically residential section of Hue, across the Perfume River from the Old City (*see also* Citadel).

NLF: *see* National Liberation Front.

NVA: North Vietnamese Army.

Operation Niagara: code name for the saturation bombing of the area surrounding Khe Sanh.

Operation Pegasus: code name for the Khe Sanh relief operation.

PAVN: People's Army of (North) Vietnam; used interchangeably with NVA, that is, North Vietnamese Army.

platoon: a subdivision of a tactical unit such as a company, usually commanded by a lieutenant.

Politburo: decision-making body of the North Vietnamese government in Hanoi.

reaction force: a military unit established specifically to counter or react to enemy action.

regiment: a military unit larger than a battalion and smaller than a division.

Regional Force: South Vietnamese regional defense unit.

Republic of Vietnam: South Vietnam.

Resolution 15: a policy statement issued by the NLF that changed the Communists' strategy toward South Vietnam from a "political struggle" to an "armed struggle."

rigor mortis: temporary stiffening of muscles occurring after death.

Rockpile: a U.S. firebase east of Khe Sanh.

Route 9: the main through road from Laos to the key cities of Quang Tri and Hue.

safe house: a place of refuge for one engaged in secret activities, such as a member of the Vietcong in South Vietnam.

Saigon: former capital of South Vietnam; renamed Ho Chi Minh City after Communist conquest.

sampan: a flat-bottomed Chinese boat usually propelled by two short oars.

sapper: an NVA/VC commando raider skilled at penetrating enemy defenses.

Seabee: a navy construction battalion (CB), or a member thereof.

section: a tactical unit of the army and marine corps smaller than a platoon and larger than a squad.

set piece: a precisely planned and executed military operation.

Silver Star: third-highest U.S. award for bravery.

Sky Spot: code name for the aerial computer control center used to coordinate aircraft operations over Khe Sanh during Operation Niagara.

South Vietnamese Military Security Service: the South Vietnamese intelligence/counterintelligence service.

Special Forces: U.S. soldiers trained in guerrilla fighting; popularly known as the Green Berets.

squad: a small party of soldiers grouped for tactical or other purposes.

strategy: the planning and directing of the entire operation of a war or campaign (*see also* tactics).

tactics: the art of placing or maneuvering forces skillfully in a battle (*see also* strategy).

TAOR: tactical area of responsibility.

Task Force X-Ray: marine command at Phu Bai responsible for operations in the area from Hai Van Pass to the northern boundary of the 1st Marine Division's TAOR.

TCK-TKN: acronym for *Tong Cong Kich, Tong Khai Nghia*, Vietnamese for "General Offensive, General Uprising"; North Vietnam's grand battle plan designed to force America's withdrawal from Vietnam and the collapse of the South Vietnamese government; more popularly known as the Tet Offensive.

Tet: lunar New Year, the most important Vietnamese holiday.

III MAF: the Third Marine Amphibious Force; commanded marines operating in I Corps sector.

TOC: tactical operations center.

trench: a ditch to protect soldiers from gunfire.

VC: *see* Vietcong.

Vietcong: a contraction of *Vietnam Cong San* (Vietnamese Communist); originally a derogatory term for Communists in the South, in use since 1956; a Communist guerrilla fighter; the military arm of the National Liberation Front.

For Further Reading

Philip Caputo, *A Rumor of War.* New York: Holt, Rinehart and Winston, 1977. A personal memoir of sixteen months in Vietnam by a young marine platoon leader.

John L. Del Vecchio, *The 13th Valley.* New York: Bantam Books, Inc., 1982. A novel considered by many to be the finest work of fiction to come out of the Vietnam War; written by an army combat correspondent who received the Bronze Star in 1971 for Heroism in Ground Action while serving with 101st Airborne Division.

Frederick Downs, *The Killing Zone: My Life in the Vietnam War.* New York: Berkley Books, 1983. The story of Platoon Delta One-Six by its platoon leader.

Edward Doyle, Samuel Lipsman, and the editors of Boston Publishing Company, *The Vietnam Experience: America Takes Over 1965–67.* Boston: Boston Publishing Company, 1982. An amply illustrated and well-written overview of America's growing involvement in the Vietnam War in the years 1965 to 1967.

Peter Goldman and Tony Fuller et al., *Charlie Company: What Vietnam Did to Us.* New York: William Morrow and Company, Inc., 1983. This book tells how the war affected sixty-five combat infantrymen who soldiered with Charlie Company in the late 1960s, showing the pain of war extending far beyond the battlefield.

Paul Johnson, *Modern Times: The World from the Twenties to the Nineties.* New York: HarperCollins Publishers, 1991. The author presents a sweeping view of American history, from the post–World War I period to the present, including a captivating section about the turbulent era of the Vietnam War.

Samuel Lipsman, Edward Doyle, and the editors of Boston Publishing Company, *The Vietnam Experience: Fighting for Time.* Boston: Boston Publishing Company, 1983. This volume of the Vietnam Experience series deals with the two years following the Tet Offensive—increasing American resistance to an ever-widening war in Vietnam; well written and illustrated.

Terrence Maitland, Peter McInerney, and the editors of Boston Publishing Company, *The Vietnam Experience: A Contagion of War.* Boston: Boston Publishing Company, 1983. A companion volume to *America Takes Over* in the Vietnam Experience series. This volume deals more with tactics than strategy, focusing on what the war in Vietnam meant to those who fought it.

Tom Mangold and John Penycate, *The Tunnels of Cu Chi.* New York: Berkley Books, 1986. A nerve-twisting account of one of the more remarkable yet little-known campaigns of the Vietnam War, fought underground in the two-hundred-mile tunnel network around Saigon between American "Tunnel Rats" and the Vietcong.

Harold G. Moore and Joseph L. Galloway, *We Were Soldiers Once . . . And Young: Ia Drang—The Battle That Changed the War in Vietnam.* New York: Random House, 1992. A powerful story of self-sacrifice and heroism during one of the most savage and significant battles of the Vietnam War, told by a battalion commander and a war correspondent who were there.

Leonard Scott, *Charlie Mike.* New York: Ballantine Books, 1985. A superb story—fictional but factual—of the infantry in action in Vietnam, told by a decorated, former rifle platoon leader in the 173rd Airborne and 75th Rangers.

Works Consulted

Robert B. Asprey, *War in the Shadows: The Guerrilla in History.* 2 vols. Garden City, NY: Doubleday & Company, Inc., 1975. Hailed as the most extensive work on guerrilla warfare ever written, this finely crafted book includes valuable information about the Vietcong and the Tet Offensive.

Mark Baker, *Nam: The Vietnam War in the Words of the Men and Women Who Fought There.* New York: Berkley Books, 1983. An oral history of the war, in the voices of those who put their lives on the line in Vietnam.

Tom Bartlett, "Tet; Bloody Tet . . .," *Leatherneck*, February 1973, pp. 16–21. A concise, well-illustrated overview of the Tet Offensive from a marine perspective.

Ray Bonds, ed., *The Vietnam War: The Illustrated History of the Conflict in Southeast Asia.* New York: Crown Publishers, Inc., 1983. Filled with action photographs, maps, and diagrams, this excellently written history contains a battle-by-battle analysis of more than thirty years of open warfare in Southeast Asia.

R. D. Camp with Eric Hammel, *Lima-6.* New York: Pocket Books, 1989. Author Camp reveals in detail and candor what it is like to be a marine officer in battle: making decisions under fire, seeing men die as a result of one's own orders, building morale, and witnessing the incredible courage of fellow marines.

Tom Carhart, *Battlefront Vietnam.* New York: Warner Books, Inc., 1991. Carhart, a former infantry platoon leader with the 101st Airborne Division in Vietnam, authoritatively reveals how American tactics and firepower won battle after battle—and why the North Vietnamese still won the war.

G. R. Christmas, "A Company Commander Reflects on Operation Hue City," *Marine Corps Gazette,* April 1971, pp. 34–39. The company commander of Hotel Company, 2nd Battalion, 5th Marines, recalls that the "best lesson learned" during the battle for Hue "was that imagination and aggressiveness are the best weapons in a commander's arsenal."

———, "A Company Commander Remembers the Battle for Hue," *Marine Corps Gazette,* February 1977, pp. 19–26. Hotel Company's commander reflects on infantry tactics and techniques used during the house-to-house fighting for Hue.

Phillip B. Davidson, *Vietnam at War: The History 1946–1975.* New York: Oxford University Press, 1988. General Westmoreland's former intelligence chief follows the entire course of the Vietnam War, from the initial French skirmishes in 1946 to the dramatic fall of Saigon in 1975. Westmoreland called this volume "must reading."

Clark Dougan, Stephen Weiss, and the editors of Boston Publishing Company, *The Vietnam Experience: Nineteen Sixty-Eight.* Boston: Boston Publishing Company, 1983. This volume, one of an excellent series on the Vietnam War, concentrates on the year when American fortunes in Vietnam began a downhill spiral; it contains detailed descriptions of the siege at Khe Sanh, the Tet Offensive, and the battle for Hue.

Frances FitzGerald, *Fire in the Lake: The Vietnamese and the Americans in Vietnam.* Boston: Little, Brown and Company, 1972. One of the first—and still one of the best—accounts of America's involvement in Vietnam, written by a freelance journalist who went to Vietnam in 1966 to report the war.

Eric Hammel, *The Siege of Khe Sanh: An Oral History.* New York: Warner Books, Inc., 1990. The first-person accounts of the men who fought and survived the terrifying siege of Khe Sanh, assembled and presented by an award-winning military historian.

Richard G. Harris, "Khe Sanh," *American History Illustrated*, March/April 1993, pp. 39–49, 71, 73. A look at the purpose and significance of the bloody eleven-week siege of Khe Sanh written a quarter century after the event.

Stanley Karnow, *Vietnam: A History*. New York: Viking, 1991. A classic account of America's war in Vietnam, written by a distinguished journalist, editor, and author; rich in detail, with a sure grasp of the issues surrounding American involvement in Vietnam.

Charles H. Krohn, *The Lost Battalion: Controversy and Casualties in the Battle of Hue*. Westport, CT: Praeger Publishers, 1993. The story of an obscure battle fought outside Hue by the 2nd Battalion of the 1st Air Cavalry Division's 12th Cavalry during the Tet Offensive. The author served as intelligence officer for the "lost battalion," before transferring to the infantry in Vietnam.

Michael Lee Lanning and Dan Cragg, *Inside the VC and the NVA: The Real Story of North Vietnam's Armed Forces*. New York: Fawcett Columbine, 1992. Two American infantry veterans of the Vietnam War team up to produce a rare book about the war as seen from the enemy's perspective.

Robert Leckie, *The Wars of America*. Vol. 2. New York: HarperPerennial, 1993. A comprehensive recounting of America's conflicts from the First World War to the Persian Gulf War; Leckie, a noted military historian, includes a brief but useful narrative of the Vietnam War and the Tet Offensive.

Bruce Martin, "House to House," *Leatherneck*, May 1968, pp. 54–57, 88. A marine's photo-essay of the house-to-house fighting in Hue during the Tet Offensive.

John Martin, "Khe Sanh," *Leatherneck*, July 1968, pp. 34–39. An active-duty marine photo-journalist reports on Khe Sanh in words and pictures at the time of the siege.

Keith William Nolan, *Battle for Hue: Tet, 1968*. Novato, CA: Presidio Press, 1983. The definitive account of the battle for Hue; Nolan writes compellingly, accurately, and with a keen eye and ear for both the comedy and tragedy of war.

————, "Khe Sanh," *Leatherneck*, December 1981. A brief, stirring account of the marines' defense of Khe Sanh.

Tim Page and John Pimlott, consulting editors, *Nam: The Vietnam Experience 1965–1975*. New York: Mallard Press, 1990. A master volume on the Vietnam era, containing specially commissioned chapters written by men who were there; includes a wealth of fine photographs, illustrations, and maps to enhance the reader's understanding of America's unwanted war; unmatched in its scope.

John Pimlott, *Vietnam: The Decisive Battles*. New York: Macmillan Publishing Company, 1990. Contains vivid accounts of seventeen major battles, well written and enhanced by photographs, illustrations, and computer graphics; includes sections on Khe Sanh and the Tet Offensive.

John Prados and Ray W. Stubbe, *Valley of Decision: The Siege of Khe Sanh*. New York: Dell Publishing, 1991. A noble achievement that lays bare the complete story of the siege at Khe Sanh, while re-creating the entire Vietnam experience in riveting prose. Written by the Lutheran chaplain of the 1st Battalion, 26th Marines, and a professional historian and analyst of internal security affairs, the book stands unsurpassed as the definitive account of seventy-seven days at Khe Sanh.

John Quick, *Dictionary of Weapons & Military Terms*. New York: McGraw-Hill, Inc., 1973. A comprehensive record of the significant weapons developed over the centuries by armies all over the world.

Neil Sheehan, *A Bright Shining Lie: John Paul Vann and America in Vietnam.* New York: Vintage Books, 1989. Winner of the National Book Award and the Pulitzer Prize for nonfiction, this masterful work tells the story of the charismatic soldier John Vann— "the one irreplaceable American in Vietnam"—and of the tragedy called the Vietnam War; absolutely must reading for those interested in learning the reality of America's war in that far place.

Edwin H. Simmons, *The Illustrated History of the Marines: The Vietnam War.* New York: Bantam Books, 1987. Simmons, a retired marine general and former commander of the 9th Marines in Vietnam, offers a brief, illustrated history of the marines in the Vietnam War; brief but interesting.

Howard R. Simpson, *Dien Bien Phu: The Epic Battle America Forgot.* New York: Brassey's Inc., 1994. An in-depth study of one of history's great battles, one that led to America's involvement in Vietnam; written by a U.S. Information Agency correspondent who shared food, wine, and danger with the doomed French soldiers at Dien Bien Phu.

Harry G. Summers Jr., *Vietnam War Almanac.* New York: Facts On File Publications, 1985. A well-researched and well-written chronicle and encyclopedia of the Vietnam War, written by a former colonel of infantry in Vietnam.

Mark A. Swearengen, "Siege: Forty Days at Khe Sanh," *Marine Corps Gazette,* April 1973, pp. 23–28. An analysis of the lessons learned at Khe Sanh for historians and future commanders.

James R. Wilson, *Landing Zones: Combat Vets from America's Proud, Fighting South Remember Vietnam.* New York: Pocket Books, 1993. An oral history of the Vietnam War, told by twenty-four soldiers from the American South, compiled and arranged by a journalist, editor, and teacher who served as a staff officer in Vietnam.

Index

Picture Credits

Cover photo: Library of Congress

AP/Wide World Photos, 23 (bottom), 41, 43 (bottom), 46

Archive Photos, 12 (bottom), 14, 20, 27, 31 (middle and bottom), 58, 75 (top), 79, 80

Corbis-Bettmann, 62 (top)

National Archives, 12 (top), 16, 17, 19, 21, 25 (bottom), 31 (top), 32, 36, 37, 43 (top), 54, 59 (both), 61, 62 (bottom), 65, 66 (both), 68, 70, 71, 76, 81, 82

UPI/Bettmann, 49

UPI/Corbis-Bettmann, 23 (top), 25 (top), 40, 45, 47, 50, 52, 56 (all), 73, 75 (bottom), 77

About the Author

Earle Rice Jr. attended San Jose City College and Foothill College on the San Francisco peninsula, after serving nine years with the U. S. Marine Corps.

He has authored twelve previous books for young adults, including fast-action fiction and adaptations of *Dracula* and *All Quiet on the Western Front.* Mr. Rice has written several books for Lucent, including *The Cuban Revolution, The Battle of Britain, The Battle of Midway,* and *The Attack on Pearl Harbor.* He has also written articles and short stories and has previously worked for several years as a technical writer.

Mr. Rice is a former senior design engineer in the aerospace industry, who now devotes full time to his writing. He lives in Julian, California, with his wife, daughter, two granddaugthers, five cats, and a dog.